No...I Won't Go There

When We Understand Who We Are in Christ We Will Not Allow Our Mind to Fulfill the Temptation to Sin

Blessings on you!

Donald H. Ledbetter

Donald H. Ledbetter, Th.D.

ISBN 978-1-0980-9579-6 (paperback)
ISBN 978-1-0980-9580-2 (digital)

Christian Faith Publishing, Inc.
832 Park Avenue
Meadville, PA 16335
www.christianfaithpublishing.com

Unless otherwise stated, all scriptures are in the New King James version of the Bible.

Printed in the United States of America

ENDORSEMENTS

Who controls the sin in your life? Do you control your sin or does your sin control you? According to Romans 6:8-14 ("For sin shall no longer be your master, because you are not under the law, but under grace"-verse14) sin enslaves man. Although many people will insist that they control their sins, the truth is that they are slaves to the power and influence of sin in their lives. In time sin takes over a person's life leaving the individual broken and alone without any real power to succeed or move forward in their lives.

Does God, the Father of Jesus Christ, have an answer to this huge dilemma? The answer is YES. God set into place before the foundations of the world an amazing plan for dealing with the impact of man's sin. He provided the means for personal salvation and freedom from the power of sin through the shed blood of His son, Jesus of Nazareth. Those who follow Jesus in faith have the potential of living a life where sin does not have to control their actions, thoughts, and motives.

Discovering that kind of freedom is what Donald Ledbetter's book *No... I Won't Go There* is all about. In his book Dr. Ledbetter shares his personal story of discovering God's plan for victory in his life as he battled his own sin nature. Out of brokenness Dr. Ledbetter discovered a better way. Built on the foundation of Romans 6 & 8 he lays out God's plan for personal victory over sin.

As you read *No... I Won't Go There* be prepared to face your own sinful nature. Be prepared to discover a new way of living the victorious Christian life. Be prepared to be challenged to live the life God intended you to live!

Dr. Randy Bennett
Director of Missions,
Kern County Southern Baptist Association
Adjunct Professor, Midwestern Seminary
Professor, Rockbridge Seminary

Many Christians find their Christian walk frustrating, powerless, and ineffective in the battle with sin. These believers lack the understanding of the power of God's Holy Spirit to provide victory in those battles.

Dr. Ledbetter's biblical and practical teaching in "No, I Won't Go There" can draw believers into a Holy Spirt filled walk of victory. I encourage church pastors and leaders to read this book and use it's teaching on Holy Spirit filled living as a tool to help believers learn the power living within them.

Kevin K. White
Executive Director
Nevada Baptist Convention

To all believers in Jesus, that this book may assist them in understanding who they are in Him.

CONTENTS

ACKNOWLEDGMENTS

———— ⌘ ————

I want to thank God for the privilege of sharing part of my life through this book. It has been through the grace and mercy of God I was privileged to learn the lessons shared in these pages. And I give praise and thanksgiving to Him for His kindness, patience, and goodness to me in allowing me to continue to learn.

The one person who has shared these experiences and has loved and encouraged me in writing this book is my dear wife, Lois. She not only lived these lessons learned with me but lived through the hard times because I had not learned them. For this, I love and appreciate her and regret I did not apprehend them sooner. She has edited the manuscript and suggested the name for the title. Without her, the book would not have been written.

We have three children, five grandchildren, and three great-grandchildren. Donna Rapp and her husband, Harold, have two children and three grandchildren; Kristen Hicks and her husband, Ben, and their children Piper, Avery, and Jedidiah; and Andrew Rapp and his wife, Dalton. Deborah May and her husband, Brian, have two daughters, Emily and Lindy. Our son Daniel and his wife, Mary, and his son, Graysen, round out our family. Had I learned these lessons earlier in my life, I think I could have been a better husband, father, and grandfather. I dearly love our family with all my heart. My prayer is for their understanding of these amazing truths and how they may bless their lives as they have mine, giving hope, peace, joy, comfort, and love in the midst of all kinds of circumstances.

Friends are very important in all of our lives. When long-time friends Roy and Nancy Owen suggested I write this book, it was what I needed to push me over the edge and begin to write. Their suggestions and encouragement have been a great blessing. When I would get stymied, they would ask how I was doing, which caused me to try again.

Another friend, Dr. Randy Bennett, has been invaluable helping with encouragement and the editing of the book. He is the Director of Missions for the Kern County Southern Baptist Association and also serves as a part-time professor in two seminaries. He is accustomed to grading doctoral dissertations, so he was a great resource in editing.

I want to thank the many friends in the churches with whom I have been privileged to minister all across the United States of America. All of them contributed to my learning and understanding of who we are in Christ and how to say no to our old sin nature.

PREFACE

The motivation for this writing comes from more than sixty years in the preaching and pastoral ministry. I surrendered to the call of God to preach the gospel in March of 1956. Since answering that call, I have been privileged to pastor four churches in Texas, California, and Nevada; serve all the Southern Baptist churches in the Nevada Baptist Convention as the director of evangelism and stewardship for eighteen years; and serve as interim pastor for a dozen different churches in Nevada and California. Also, I want to leave something tangible for my children, friends, and churches concerning some of the rich and important truths of living a joyous, peaceful, and happy Christian life in a world filled with unpleasant circumstances. The Christian life is a continuous process of learning to be more like Jesus. I make no claim to have attained or learned everything about the Christian life. However, had I learned the truths I am sharing at an earlier age, I think I could have been a better person, friend, husband, father, and pastor. We can all thank God for His grace and mercy as well as the patience He shows us in our progressive sanctification, which is our step-by-step spiritual growth in Christ.

It is through multiple stumbles, blunders, failures, and some blessed victories that I have learned these truths, and allowed God to teach me through His mercy. As the scripture says, *"Through the Lord's mercies we are not consumed, because His compassions fail not. They are new every morning; Great is Your faithfulness"* (Lam. 3:22–23).

God is always working with each of us to become a person who allows Jesus to live His life through us. We can thank Him for His forgiveness and love. Through all the years of ministry experience, I have come to the conclusion that many, if not most, believers in our churches know very little of who they are in Christ and know even less of what it means to live the Christian life from the position of victory over the power of sin and temptations.

In this writing we will explore what happens to us when we become a believer and how Jesus expects us to allow Him to be our life. We will discover how, in our sin-cursed world, Jesus offers us joy, peace, and victory in the midst of difficult and trying circumstances. We will look at how God desires and expects us to have a daily intimate relationship with Him. This relationship will focus on how we become more intimate with Jesus every day. We will see how this is possible and can become a living reality every day of our lives. We will explore what it means to trust the Lord with all our hearts and not to lean on our own understanding, and also how to acknowledge God in all we do and to trust Him to direct our lives in whatever our circumstance may be. God is always working, using every circumstance of life to sanctify us in becoming more like Jesus. Since Jesus lives within each believer in all the power of the resurrection, through God the Holy Spirit, we have the authority and power to say no to the temptations of the old wretched man.

Trust in the Lord with all your heart, And lean not on your own understanding; In all your ways acknowledge Him, And He shall direct your paths (Prov. 3:5–6).

INTRODUCTION

After one becomes a follower of Jesus, often others will ask the question, "What has happened to you?" Just as often, we do not know how to properly give an answer to the question. We know that we have had a transforming experience with Jesus that has literally changed our life. The Bible calls this experience the new birth. We have been spiritually born again. However, we do not know exactly how to explain it to someone else or how we are going to live this new life in Christ. We ask ourselves, "What do I do now?" or "How do I live this new life in Christ?"

Those of us saved in a Bible-believing, Bible-preaching church believe we are saved by grace. However, most of the time we act as if we are saved and sanctified by good works. From my experience in working with many different churches, I have learned the greatest need is for individual believers to have an intimate personal relationship with Jesus every day. By nature we think in order to grow we must do something. In reality we need to learn to rest or abide in Christ and seek His will for our lives and allow Him to direct our good works. When our activity comes out of our relationship with Christ, pastors and church members cease to be burned out from serving in the energy of fleshly efforts.

In many of our modern churches, we attempt to live by a set of rules to grow in our new relationship with Jesus. These rules may say we must begin to read our Bible and pray every day, we must be faithful to attend church meetings each week, and to begin to give to the church regularly, etc.

Although these disciplines are essential for our spiritual growth, unless they are motivated by our personal intimate relationship with God through Jesus, they become laborious and meaningless. We find ourselves trying to live the Christian life by our fleshly efforts and throw up our hands in futility because we fail. However, it is not God's will for us to fail. He desires for us to allow Jesus to live His life in and through us each day. Jesus said we must deny ourselves daily and follow Him. This means we are to yield ourselves completely to Jesus and His control daily. Jeremiah shared what God says about this in Jeremiah 9:23–24:

> *Thus says the Lord: "Let not the wise man glory in his wisdom, let not the mighty man glory in his might, nor let the rich man glory in his riches; but let him who glories glory in this, that he understands and knows Me, that I am the Lord, exercising lovingkindness, judgment, and righteousness in the earth. For in these I delight," says the Lord.*

We must make it our priority to know God the Father, God the Son, and God the Holy Spirit intimately every day and to glory in that relationship. Out of this growing relationship, His will is revealed to us concerning the good works He has planned for us to serve Him.

In January of 2018, Lois (my wife) and I were visiting Roy and Nancy Owen who

are longtime friends living in Reno. We were
there on Sunday, so we attended South Reno
Baptist Church with them. It was there we
first met them many years ago when we were
all members of South Reno. We attended
their Bible study class with them, which is a
large senior adult class. They were studying
the Christian life as it relates to good works
in Ephesians 2:8–10 which reads,

For by grace you have been saved through
faith, and that not of yourselves; it is the gift of
God, not of works, lest anyone should boast. For
we are His workmanship, created in Christ Jesus
for good works, which God prepared beforehand
that we should walk in them.

Most of the class concluded we are saved
by God's grace, but some of the members
seemed to struggle with how our good works
fit in. They did not seem to understand that
good works come out of their intimate relationship with Jesus.

All this time I was formatting in my
sub-conscience how all good works come out
of our relationship with Jesus. As the class
time drew to a close, the teacher asked for
comments. After everyone had their say, I
raised my hand, and under the Holy Spirit's
direction, I shared what happens when one
is saved and how good works follow. The
teacher and the class responded in a most gra-
cious manner, and when we were alone with
our friends, they encouraged me to write it

all down. The next morning before we left for home, I wrote down a rough draft. Our friends, Roy and Nancy, made copies and handed them out to their class. They also encouraged me to write this book. What I said that Sunday morning is contained in the following summary.

The following is the summary of the sevenfold spiritual process of becoming a follower of Jesus that I shared with our friends and their Sunday school class. We will explore how we came to understand that we needed a Savior, and what happened to us the moment we asked Jesus to be the Lord and Savior of our life.

1. **The message of the good news of Jesus is shared with us.**

    The message is of God's love for lost humanity as shared in John 3:16. God loves sinners and sent Jesus to pay the price for our sin so we may have everlasting life.

    For God so loved the world that He gave His only begotten Son, that whosoever believes in Him shall not perish, but have everlasting life. (John 3:16)

2. **The details of our salvation experience begin with the grace of God.**

    Through the mercy of God and by His grace we read, or someone tells us, about God's love in sending Jesus to die on Calvary's cross for our sin. All of mankind is guilty of sin. We have all sinned (said I will against God's will) and have come short of God's glory. Grace means God extended His unmerited favor to us. There is nothing we can do to save ourselves or have we or can we do anything to deserve to be forgiven of our sin. It is only by God's love and grace.

For by grace you have been saved through faith, and that not of yourselves; it is the gift of God, not of works, lest anyone should boast. For we are His workmanship, created in Christ Jesus for good works, which God prepared beforehand that we should walk in them. (Eph. 2:8–10)

3. **God the Father draws us to Jesus (God the Son) through God the Holy Spirit.**

   The Holy Spirit begins a process of drawing a person to the Father after hearing about the cross. The Father, the Son, and the Holy Spirit are all working together in the salvation experience. No one comes to the Father without the drawing of the Holy Spirit.

   No one can come to Me unless the Father who sent Me draws him. (John 6:44)

4. **God the Holy Spirit convicts us of sin and convinces us of the truth of the death and resurrection of Jesus.**

   When Jesus was preparing His apostles for His departure, He promised the coming of the Holy Spirit who convicts of sin, righteousness, and judgment.

*It is to your advantage that I go away; for
if I do not go away, the Helper will not come to
you; but if I depart, I will send Him to you. And
when He has come, He will convict the world
of sin, and of righteousness, and of judgment.*
(John 16:7–8)

As the Holy Spirit draws us to the Father, He also
brings conviction of the sinful nature and then convinces of the truth of the message of the cross. Without
this experience, it is impossible to be forgiven of sin.

5. **God the Holy Spirit places us spiritually into the
death of Jesus on the cross.**
Paul tells us we are baptized into the body of
Christ by the Holy Spirit.

*For by one Spirit we were all baptized into
one body.* (1 Cor. 12:13)

The Holy Spirit draws us to the Father, convicting us of our sin and convincing us of God's love for
us. At the moment of faith, the Holy Spirit immerses
us into the death of Jesus on the cross. This is the baptism by the Holy Spirit. We are crucified spiritually
with Christ and spiritually die to the power of the sin
nature. When the temptations of our sinful nature
come to our mind, because the power of the Holy
Spirit lives in us, we can say no to the temptation. The
power of our old sin nature is replaced by the Holy
Spirit.

But now having been set free from sin, and having become slaves of God, you have your fruit to holiness, and the end, everlasting life. (Rom. 6:22)

Paul is saying we have been set free from the hold the old sin nature had on us. The old sinful nature becomes subservient to Jesus who lives in us through the person of the Holy Spirit. The resurrected Christ lives in us with all of the power it took for Him to come out of the grave.

6. **A lifelong progression of sanctification, which means becoming more like Jesus, now begins.**

I can do all things through Christ who strengthens me. (Phil. 4:13)

The only way we can live the Christian life is to allow Jesus to live His life within us. We can do all things through His strength within us. It is impossible to grow in God's grace through the efforts of the fleshly nature. An example of fleshly efforts would be vowing to be more disciplined in prayer and Bible study so we might seem more spiritual to other people. We might try to get up earlier in the morning and read the Bible and pray with a goal of drawing closer to Jesus. However, unless these good intentions are motivated by our intimate relationship with Jesus and being in His will, failure will result. We end up trying to do a good thing for the wrong reason.

NO...I WON'T GO THERE

As a young Christian, I read books and heard stories of successful preachers who were up early in the morning to read the Bible and pray. They were touted as great men of God. I was sincere and wanted to be used by God. I wanted to be a great man of God. When I arrived at seminary, I started getting up early to spend time in prayer. I worked for the seminary and had the responsibility of opening the buildings and making sure everything was ready for the day. This gave me the opportunity to arrive early and get in a room by myself and pray before I started work. After a period of time, I gave up on the effort. I was doing it through the efforts of the flesh and not under the direction of the Holy Spirit; therefore, I physically wore out. When we try to do spiritual work in our own strength, we wear out.

7. **A life of good works is directed by Jesus.**

For we are His workmanship, created in Christ Jesus for good works, which God prepared beforehand that we should walk in them. (Eph. 2:10)

Through God's grace we are forgiven our sin and given the free gift of salvation. As we abide daily in the presence of Jesus, our activities will be directed out of that relationship. The desire of the heart will be to know and live in the will of God. Out of the position of rest, we are led to the work God wants us to do. This means we must learn to wait on God for instruction before doing anything.

Understanding the sevenfold process for coming to know the Lord has been a life-changing experience. As wonderful as it is, there is so much more believers can expect to happen in their lives. The question that comes to mind is, "What comes next?" As believers of Christ, we look to the Bible to discover the next steps. In chapter 1 we will take a look at the two steps every new believer in the New Testament followed during the early days of their faith.

Chapters 2 through 7 will address the critical mileposts every believer faces throughout the journey of following the Lord. Chapter 2 deals with the inner battle between the old life and the new life in Christ. Chapter 3 deals with the importance of the baptism and filling by the Holy Spirit. Chapter 4 deals with the three sins believers commit against the Holy Spirit. Chapter 5 teaches how to live from the position of victory. Chapter 6 deals with how we can escape temptation. Chapter 7 closes out the book with how Jesus becomes our life.

First we will look at how the church in Jerusalem set the pattern for Christians and the church through the ages for reaching the unsaved multitudes and growing and maturing in Christ.

CHAPTER 1

***

The Early Days of Our Faith

Some of the last words of Jesus were recorded in Matthew 28:19–20, which is generally referred to as the Great Commission. Here He tells believers to go into all the world and make disciples of all nations. This included sharing a threefold message, the cross, baptizing those who believe, and teaching those who believe to obey all His commands.

> *Go therefore and make disciples of all the nations, baptizing them in the name of the Father and of the Son and of the Holy Spirit, teaching them to observe all things that I have commanded you; and lo, I am with you always, even to the end of the age. (Matt. 28:19–20)*

Jesus established a threefold pattern for the New Testament church. Evangelize the unbeliever, baptize the new believer, and then instruct them to observe His teachings. The Great Commission set the pattern.

Many years ago, as a college student I began to learn a lesson that has stayed with me through the years. I got a job as a carpenter's helper. This was before the days of power saws and precut two-by-four studs. We had to cut them with an old-fashioned hand saw. The old master carpenter carefully measured the length of the two-by-four stud he said we needed. Then he did a strange thing (at least I thought it was strange). He named it Pat. Being a not-so-bright college student, I asked him why he named it Pat and not something else. He said, "This is our pattern. We must use the pattern to measure or mark off the remainder of the two-by-four studs." Being as bright as I was, I soon figured out it would be a lot faster if we used the last one we cut to measure the next one. Therefore, I showed my ignorance and asked him why we did not save some time.

He was patient with me and explained if we did it like I suggested, every one of the boards would be one saw width longer than the one before. The wall would slant upward. Every two-by-four stud had to be measured by the pattern. Several years later I was reminded of this lesson. I had an occasion to build a wall in the basement of the parsonage, and I had to cut them to a special length. I had forgotten the lesson I thought I had learned and cut them like I had suggested earlier. When I tried to put it in place, it would not fit. One end was longer than the other, and it slanted upward. Then it hit me—I had not used the pattern. Neither had I remembered the lesson I thought I had learned many years before. Likewise, our Christian faith must be measured by the first-century church in Jerusalem, which set the pattern.

The Pattern of the New Testament Reveals Expectations

In Acts 2, the expectations are laid out for the new believer. After we receive Jesus as our personal Savior, we are to follow Him in believer's baptism. Then we are to begin a lifelong study of the teachings the apostles taught about Jesus and the Christian life. We are to continue in prayer and fellowship with other believers ministering to the needs of others, all the while sharing the love of Jesus with lost humanity seeking to lead them to a saving faith in Him. All of this enhances our spiritual growth and maturing process, which is part of the expectations.

Paul called the churches back from a salvation of works and law-keeping. Peter called the churches back to a proper view of suffering. John called the churches back to the pattern, warning against false teachers.

The church in Jerusalem set the original pattern of what is expected of new believers. It is a twofold pattern of baptism and instruction.

They taught sinners needed to be saved and baptized because they had been saved, and then they were added to the membership of the church. In Acts 2 we read about the day of the Feast of Pentecost. It was the day when God fulfilled the prophecy of the baptism by the Holy Spirit. Multitudes were gathered in Jerusalem for the feast, and the Holy Spirit filled the church, and they preached the message of Jesus to the crowds in their own languages. The Holy Spirit had come to indwell the church. It was also the day when Simon Peter was given a second chance. It was only a few weeks before that he denied he knew Jesus. This was when Jesus was being falsely tried and sentenced to die for our sins on the cross. Peter denied the Lord three times. Now he is filled with the Holy Spirit and preaches with great power and understanding concerning all Jesus did for mankind. Peter was given a second chance. There are times when we need second chances, and God, through His love and mercy, grants it to us as He did Peter. Peter preached how Jesus died for sin and was resurrected victorious over sin and the grave. He cried out for them to be saved, and three thousand received Jesus as their personal Savior and were baptized.

"Then those who gladly received his word were baptized; and that day about three thousand souls were added to them" (Acts 2:41).

Those added to the church were taught the apostles' doctrine, and they continued in fellowship and witnessing to the unsaved. God added to the church daily those who were being saved. This set the pattern for the beginning of the Christian life and the New Testament church. We will now look with more detail at the two-step pattern.

Step 1: Those who were saved and baptized were added to the church.

They were added to the local church in Jerusalem. Every new believer became a part of the local church. The word *church* is translated from the Greek word *ekklesia*. The term meant a convened assembly set apart for a specific purpose. According to Dr. Fred Fisher, my New Testament professor at Golden Gate Baptist Theological Seminary, "The New Testament Christians thought of themselves as representing or embodying Christ in the work of calling men to repentance and loyalty to the living Lord. This would indicate that when *ekklesia* is used it refers to a local assembly of God's people in some aspect of their life."[1]

Dr. Fisher goes on to say that in the New Testament, *ekklesia* is always used with an immediate or ultimate reference to the local congregation in some phase of its existence and life. Ninety out 108 times used it is clearly local. That is 83 percent of the time. There are eighteen times when it is not as clear, but a close study reveals that they are referring to the local assembly. Those who were saved were baptized.[2]

Baptism is an act of obedience that publicly professes one's faith in Jesus. A test of whether a person is a true follower of Jesus is his or her obedience to Jesus's commands. The new believer is to be baptized by the authority of a local New Testament church.

> *Now by this we know that we know Him, if we keep His commandments. He who says, "I know Him," and does not keep His commandments, is a liar, and the truth is not in him. But whoever keeps His word, truly the love of God is perfected in him. By this we know that we are in Him. (1 John 2:3–5)*

If we have been truly converted to Jesus, we will want to be obedient. Jesus commanded us to be baptized. Our baptism

---

[1]   Fred L. Fisher, *The Church: A New Testament Study* (Unpublished manuscript, 1961), 14.
[2]   Ibid.

symbolizes our being immersed spiritually into the death of Jesus on the cross.

At that moment we are freed from the bondage of the sin nature and given the power of the resurrected Jesus through the Holy Spirit. Our baptism also symbolizes our identification with the resurrection of Jesus and His indwelling us through the Holy Spirit. Jesus lives within us with all the power it took to raise Him from the grave. This water baptism is symbolic of the baptism by the Holy Spirit. It is essential for us to understand these truths. They reveal who we are in Christ, which enables us to live from the position of victory.

"Go therefore and make disciples of all the nations, baptizing them in the name of the Father and of the Son and of the Holy Spirit..." (Matt. 28:19).

Jesus gave the Great Commission to the church to baptize new believers and to instruct them in living the Christian life. This was not a suggestion or an option for His followers. In the New Testament, believers were baptized. Philip baptized the Ethiopian eunuch in Acts 8:3. When Paul was saved, he was baptized in Acts 9:18. Cornelius and his company were baptized in Acts 10:47–48.

Step 2: These new believers continued in the apostles' doctrine, fellowship, and prayer.

> *And they continued steadfastly in the apostles' doctrine and fellowship, in the breaking of bread, and in prayers. Then fear came upon every soul, and many wonders and signs were done through the apostles. Now all who believed were together, and had all things in common, and sold their possessions and goods,*

*and divided them among all, as anyone had
need. So continuing daily with one accord in
the temple, and breaking bread from house to
house, they ate their food with gladness and
simplicity of heart, praising God and having
favor with all the people. And the Lord added
to the church daily those who were being saved.*
(Acts 2:42–47)

The second part of the pattern is continued in these verses.
This church fulfilled the second part of the twofold pattern
with study and learning. There were three thousand new believers who sat at the feet of the apostles and learned about their
new life in Christ. They had been baptized and now were learning about the importance of fellowship, prayer, giving, and the
truths we will look at in the remaining pages of this book. Also,
it is apparent they were excited about sharing their newfound
faith with others as the Lord added to the church daily those
who were being saved. They had set the pattern for us to follow. As modern-day believers, we are to be baptized by a local
church and then allow them to instruct us in how to live the
Christian life.

What joy fills our hearts when we trust Jesus as our Lord
and Savior. At this point we mistakenly think we will never have
any more problems. However, we are just beginning to live the
Christian life. We are newborn spiritual babies and have a life-
time of growing up ahead of us learning how Jesus is to be our
life. The battle with the old sin nature begins which is a part of
our progression of becoming more like Jesus.

CHAPTER 2

Expect an Ongoing Inner Battle

It is amazing what takes place in our hearts when we believe in Jesus and trust Him as our personal Savior. Jesus comes into our lives and transforms us into a new person. Our sins are forgiven, and great joy and peace fills our lives. As a young pastor, my wife and I ministered six years in Elko, Nevada, before we had the privilege of seeing anyone come to Christ. After all this time it finally began to happen, people were surrendering their hearts and lives to Jesus. Joy filled their hearts and ours as well. In order to pay bills and put food on the table, I painted houses part-time. While on one of these jobs, I met a young man who was doing plumbing in the house I was working on. During the course of conversation, I shared how Jesus loved him and would forgive him of his sin. He finished his job in record time in order to get away from me. He had gotten away from me, but he could not get away from God. In a short period, both he and his wife had received Jesus as their personal Savior. Their hearts were filled with joy, and their lives were changed. They thought all their problems were solved and their old way of life would never be a problem again. Great joy and happiness had filled their hearts, and they thought they would never face another spiritual battle. However, it wasn't long until they realized there would be an ongoing inner battle with the old sin nature.

As new believers, we make new promises and commitments to God. We make decisions to put away our selfishness, anger, bitterness, lying, substance abuse, gluttony, alcohol, and lust. This list goes on and on. As new believers, we seemed to be so close to the Lord. He was a part of us everywhere we went and was the center of our thoughts. Then it seemed without warning, those feelings began to go away. The wonderful closeness with the Lord began to grow dim. We began to do some of the bad things we promised not to do. This joy and peace may last a few days, a week, a few months, or maybe longer, but then reality sets in. Someone may cross us, and before we know it, in our anger, profanity spews out of our mouth, and we wonder what is happening. What is our problem? Do other believers experience the return of bad behavior and bad attitudes? There is good news for us all. Even the amazing Paul the Apostle struggled with what the Bible calls the "old nature." We, like Paul in Romans 7, say the things I want to do I do not do, and the things I don't want to do I end up doing. *For the good that I will to do, I do not do; but the evil I will not to do, that I practice. Now if I do what I will not to do, it is no longer I who do it, but sin that dwells in me* (Rom. 7:19–20).

This was exactly what was happening to this young couple and happens to every new believer. We are all newborn spiritual babies and must be cared for and taught how to grow up in Christ. All of us have to learn how to deal with our old sin nature, and it is the responsibility of mature believers to give this care and direction.

The following is my story.

I remember as a young boy when I began to be aware of my need of Jesus, my heart became burdened and heavy because of the conviction of my sin. Although I had not lived long enough to commit a lot of bad sinful things, I knew I was a sinner, and something was wrong between me and God. I began to talk to my mother about what was wrong with me, and she explained how all of us are sinners and I needed to invite Jesus into my life. There were times I felt like I would die before I understood how to invite Jesus into my life to be my personal Savior. However, when I did, the burden was lifted, and I felt set free. Through the years, I have seen many men, women, teenagers, and children who were under conviction of their sin and were being drawn to Jesus. The pain of conviction was always on their faces, and when they said yes to Jesus, the joy was always beaming from their eyes.

After I trusted Jesus, I remember as a young boy of nine, I began to experience the inner struggle of a spiritual battle. I had received Jesus as my personal Savior. However, no one had given me any instruction on how to live this new life in Christ. Everyone said I needed to be a good boy, but I was not taught any principles, so I, as a nine-year-old, could understand how to fight the battle. As

I grew older, all I heard was I should read the Bible and pray, not do bad things, and be faithful in church attendance. All these were things I was trying to do. There was no specific instruction on how to overcome the sin nature and how the power of the resurrected Christ lived in me through the presence of the Holy Spirit. I went to college and seminary where I attained a little more understanding, but I still did not feel equipped in how to overcome the sin nature. While working as evangelism director for the Nevada Baptist Convention, I worked on committees for the Home Mission Board to develop materials to train new believers. Most of these focused on the importance of Bible study, prayer, witnessing and being faithful in church attendance. All these are important but lacking in addressing the main issue.

Looking back on these experiences, I realized as a new believer I was like a newborn baby who needs someone to care for their every need. This privilege is bestowed on parents. Although every parent feels inadequate, we do the best we know how to feed, burp, and change diapers. Everything is done to enable them to grow up healthy and complete. We teach them how to crawl, walk, and run, along with what is right and what is wrong. Newborn spiritual babes often have no one to give him or her the personal care they need for understanding who they are in

Christ. This was what I experienced. My parents did the best they knew how, but no one had taught them the truths of spiritual discipleship and growth. Our pastor was a good, loving man of God, but he was not taught to spiritually care for new believers. Therefore, I struggled trying to do what was right. The things I wanted to do I failed to do, and the things I did not want to do I did. I read everything I could find on the victorious and Spirit-filled life. Some were good and some not so good, but they motivated me to study the Scripture to find out what God said about this subject. There were two of my seminary professors who took me under their care and taught me things I had not learned. Overtime, I learned God had already provided the victory through Christ, and I needed to learn to be intimate with Him each day.

Through a daily study of the Scripture, I began to understand Jesus had already won my victory through the cross and the resurrection. It is all about Jesus. I had tried to draw closer to Jesus by the things I could do like praying, reading my Bible more, and attending church. I learned real intimacy comes through rejoicing in what He had done for me and thanking Him and praising Him in all things. Paul taught extensively on overcoming the old sin nature and the baptism and the filling of the Holy Spirit. I studied these subjects including all the theories man had come up with and found most were just theories. Always coming back to the Scripture, I concluded living in victory centered on understanding these doctrines. After years of searching, I realized that the following two questions stood out in my struggle to live the victorious Christian life.

How do I overcome the old sin nature and live from the position of victory?
How do I experience a daily intimate personal relationship with Jesus where I surrender all I am to Him every day?

These are questions every new believer needs to explore. In the rest of this chapter, we will look at two simple principles to apply to our lives in overcoming our old sin nature and experiencing a daily intimate personal relationship with Jesus. The first principle is our new identity in Christ.

1. **We Have Been Given a New Identity in Christ That Overcomes Our Sin Nature**

> *What shall we say then? Shall we continue in sin [sin nature] that grace may abound? Certainly not! How shall we who died to sin [sin nature] live any longer in it? Or do you not know that as many of us as were baptized into Christ Jesus were baptized into His death? Therefore we were buried with Him through baptism into death, that just as Christ was raised from the dead by the glory of the Father, even so we also should walk in newness of life. For if we have been united together in the likeness of His death, certainly we also shall be in the likeness of His resurrection, knowing this, that our old man was crucified with Him, that the body of sin*

might be done away with, that we should no
longer be slaves of sin. For he who has died has
been freed from sin. (Rom. 6:1–6)

In this passage, Paul has brought out two major facts. First, when God saves us, we have been delivered from the power of our old sin nature. However, at the same time, the sin nature is left in us lying dormant and will tempt us to sin. Secondly, God at the same time imparts the divine nature of Jesus, which gives us both the desire and the power to do God's will through the Holy Spirit.

This conclusion comes after many years of studying the old sin nature and the baptism by the Holy Spirt. I have pondered over this passage of scripture for years and never really fully comprehended its meaning until I studied Dr. Kenneth Wuest's commentary on this passage. (He was a longtime professor of Greek at Moody Bible Institute.) He says the key to the inter-pretation of the entire chapter is in the way the word "sin" is used. He believes every time the word "sin" is used as a noun, it refers to the evil nature in the Christian. He says when we read the following verses and substitute the words "sinful nature" for the word "sin," a clearer meaning is understood (verses 1, 2, 6, 10, 11, 13, 14, 16, 17, 18, 20, 22, 23).[3]

In Romans 6, Paul shares how Jesus has already taken care of all our needs through the cross and the resurrection. God, through His love, mercy, and grace sent His only son to expe-rience the pain and wrath of our sin, the pain and wrath we were destined to bear. When we place our faith in His death and believe He arose from the grave, we are forgiven our sin. It

---

[3] Wuest, K. S., *Wuest's Word Studies From The Greek New Testament: For The English Reader*, vol. 2 (Grand Rapids: Eerdmans, 1997), 90.

is through this identification with Jesus that we are freed from the power of our old sin nature (living life our way instead of God's way) and die to the law. By faith, we accept these facts with the assurance Christ lives in us and we live in Him through the Holy Spirit. Anytime we try to live the Christian life without understanding who we are in Christ, there will be turmoil within. Paul reminds us of three very important truths.

- **We are placed into His death.**

When Jesus died on the cross, He died for our sin. The Holy Spirit immersed us into the death of Jesus the moment we received Him as our Savior (Rom. 6:1–4). Here, we identify with Jesus in His death, and the power our old nature had over us is broken.

Also, in verses 1–4, Paul tells us how water baptism is symbolic of the Holy Spirit placing us into the death of Christ on the cross. We know this is a spiritual baptism because we learned in chapter 1 how our salvation experience always precedes water baptism (Acts 2:40–41). This is the baptism by the Holy Spirit. (The Holy Spirit spiritually immersing us into the death of Jesus.) The water baptism experience has no saving power. Water baptism is a picture of our identifying with the death, burial, and resurrection of Jesus (we will give more detail in the next chapter on the baptism by the Holy Spirit). The Holy Spirit draws us to Jesus, He convicts our sin, He convinces us of the truth of the Gospel, and as we open our heart to Jesus, the Holy Spirit baptizes (immerses us) into the death of Jesus on the cross. Our sin is covered by the blood of Jesus, and God the Father imputes the righteousness of Christ to us. We are justified by faith in Jesus. Justification means that God declares us righteous. He sees us as if we have never sinned. Jesus becomes

NO...I WON'T GO THERE

the substitute, paying the wages for sin, which is death. He pays this price to God the Father so that when He looks at us as the repentant sinner, He sees the righteousness of Jesus. Water baptism symbolizes this entire process. As believers, we should begin to learn what these truths mean in our lives soon after our conversion. When a new believer is counseled concerning the meaning of water baptism, it should include the meaning of the baptism by the Holy Spirit. When we understand these truths, we will know we have the authority to overcome the old sin nature.

- **We are placed into His resurrection.**

When Jesus died, our old sin nature was placed into His death. We died to the power of the old sin nature. Because we died spiritually with Jesus when He was resurrected, we were resurrected with Him. We were raised to walk in the newness of His life. This defines our identity in Christ. Paul explains this in Romans 6:5–6.

> *For if we have been united together in the likeness of His death, certainly we also shall be in the likeness of His resurrection, knowing this, that our old man was crucified with Him, that the body of sin might be done away with, that we should no longer be slaves of sin. For he who has died has been freed from sin.*

We have already stated how we have been crucified with Christ, but do we understand what that means? It means when Jesus was crucified, I was crucified, and you were crucified. Our hands were spread over His hands, and our feet were placed over His feet, and the nails that pierced His hands and feet pierced our hands and feet. We were crucified with Him. All our sin was nailed to His cross. Spiritually, we died with Him. Think on the meaning of this experience, and it will touch our hearts. We are in Him, and He is within us through the Holy Spirit. At this time, we die to the law (Rom. 7:4). The law is replaced by the Holy Spirit.

To die with Christ means we are separated from the power of the sinful nature. This is difficult for us to comprehend since we are alive physically. It is helpful to understand the meaning of dying with Christ to look at how the word separation is used in the Bible. In Romans 6, death means separation. The Bible speaks of four types of the separation of death. There is physical death, spiritual death, the believer's death to the sinful nature, and eternal death. We understand all these carry the meaning of separation. Physical death is our spirit's separation from our earthly body when we die physically. Spiritual death is our separation from God. Our being dead to the sinful nature is the separation of the power of the old sin nature from us as a believer. The second death or eternal death is separation from God in an eternal place called hell. This helps us understand how being dead to the sinful nature means, as a believer, we are separated from the power of the sin nature and no longer to be controlled by its power. We are no longer a slave to the sin nature; therefore, we can say no to temptation. Before we became a believer in Christ, we were a slave to the sin nature. After we become a believer in Christ, we are set free from the power of the sin nature.

Paul had asked the question, "Shall we continue in sin [*sin nature*] so that grace may abound?" In Romans. 6:2, he answers with a resounding certainly not. The power of our sinful nature is rendered helpless on the cross when we are baptized by the Holy

Spirit into the death of Christ, and our eternal relationship is established once and for all with Him. Jesus paid the price for our sin. Spiritually, the power of our old sin nature takes a back seat to Jesus when we accept Him as our personal Savior. However, it still lives within our body and is like a back seat driver trying to get us to take wrong turns in life, which breaks our fellowship with Jesus. This causes inner turmoil and conflict. The old sin nature lies dormant and has no power over us until we allow it to be plugged back into our life. It is like the light beside my chair. It has no power to give light until I plug it in. When the Holy Spirit places us into the death of Christ spiritually, we die with Him and are delivered from the power sin had over our lives. We are no longer slaves to the sin nature's power because, spiritually, we were in Christ when He was resurrected. He was raised victorious over sin. Being raised with Jesus, we have His authority empowering us to not allow our sin nature to plug back into our lives. It is imperative we learn and understand this truth in order for us to live from the position of victory. When we yield all we are to Jesus every day, we are empowered to say no to the temptation to sin. The key is realizing we must yield our will to Jesus every day.

- **Jesus comes to live in us through the person of the Holy Spirit.**

The question is often asked, "How is Jesus going to live in us as believers?" When Jesus was preparing His disciples for the time when He would no longer be with them, He promised to come to them in the person of the Holy Spirit. The following passage from John 14 reveals this truth.

And I will pray the Father, and He will give you another Helper, that He may abide with you forever—the Spirit of truth, whom the world cannot receive, because it neither sees Him nor knows Him; but you know Him, for He dwells with you and will be in you. I will not leave you orphans; I will come to you. (John 14:16–18)

The power of our sin nature died with Jesus on the cross when we trusted Him as our Savior. His life entered our bodies through the person of the Holy Spirit to live His life within us. In John 14:16–18, Jesus tells the apostles of His soon departure. He assures them of not leaving them alone. Jesus prays to the Father and asks Him to send another comforter who will be with them forever. In the Greek text, it is the word *allon*, which means "another of the same kind."[4] Jesus was saying I am going away physically so I can come to you in the person of the Holy Spirit. The Holy Spirit is the other of the same kind as Jesus. When I retired from the Nevada Baptist Convention, they gave me a black Mont Blanc pen. If someone else gave me a black Mont Blanc pen, it would be another of the same kind. It would be just like the other one. The Holy Spirit is Jesus living in us. Jesus fulfills His promise of coming to the apostles and all believers through the person of the Holy Spirit. He is the power within enabling us to yield our all to Him so we can say no to the sin nature and He never leaves us.

The second principle is being obedient to the things we should know about Jesus.

---

[4] Robertson, A. T., *Word Pictures in the New Testament (Jn 14:16)* (Nashville, TN: Broadman Press, 1933).

41

2. **Obedience to the Things We Should Know about Jesus Results in Being More Intimate with Him**

In the last forty years of ministry, I have served many churches consulting in the area of evangelism and church growth. Over half of these years also included serving as interim pastor for a period of a year or more at a time. Every church I served seemed to share the same need. They were going through the motions of living the Christian life but did not experience a daily intimate relationship with Jesus. They were not experiencing God's presence. I had gone through this process in my own life; therefore, this caused me to focus on seeking an intimate personal relationship with Jesus as I ministered to the churches. If I was not experiencing intimacy, neither would the church. Together we would be enjoying God's loving presence and were able to discern His will. I learned this relationship was achieved by being obedient to the things I knew to be true about Jesus. The first thing I learned was when times were tough or I did not know what was happening to rejoice in the Lord and to give thanks to Him in all things. When I responded in this manner, He always drew me near to Him. Then when I was worshiping, whether in a service or a lone, I would read a verse of scripture or hear a song about Jesus and be overcome with His presence. This blessed, energized, and motivated me in serving my Lord. It was a matter of being obedient to the things I knew about Jesus.

In Romans 6, Paul repeatedly talked about things we know or should know. By being obedient to the things we know, our intimacy with Jesus grows deeper. We will look at three of these.

- **We should know we are forgiven by God's grace.**

> *What shall we say then? Shall we continue in sin [sin nature] that grace may abound? Certainly not!* (Rom. 6:1)

Grace is defined as the unmerited favor of God extended to us because of His great love. We have done nothing to deserve His love and mercy. It is truly by His grace we are forgiven our sin. When we are obedient to thank Him and praise Him for grace, He draws us close to His heart. When we meditate on these truths, our hearts are warmed and blessed, and we become more intimate with Jesus. We realize without Him we are nothing and are forgiven only by His grace (Eph. 2:8–9).

- **We should know we have died to the law but are alive to God through Jesus.**

Paul tells us in Romans 7 how he would not have known what sin was without the law. When the law said thou shall not covet, he knew he was not to covet (Rom. 7:7). He had also given the example of a woman whose husband had died freeing her to marry again without committing adultery. She was free

NO...I WON'T GO THERE

because he had died (Rom. 7:2–3). We, as believers, have died to the law through the sacrifice of Jesus (Rom. 7:4).

> *Now if we died with Christ, we believe that we shall also live with Him, knowing that Christ, having been raised from the dead, dies no more. Death no longer has dominion over Him. For the death that He died, He died to sin once for all; but the life that He lives, He lives to God. Likewise you also, reckon yourselves to be dead indeed to sin, but alive to God in Christ Jesus our Lord.* (Rom. 6:8–11)

In Romans 6:8–11, Paul had affirmed if we died with Christ, we also live with Him. He based this on the fact of knowing that Christ having raised from the dead dies no more. Death no longer has dominion over Him. Then He says every believer must count on the fact he or she is dead to the power of the sin nature but alive to God. Because of our identity with Jesus, we have the same benefits He does. We are dead to the law but alive to God through Christ. Does this mean we do not keep the law? Does it mean we can now lie, covet, or commit adultery since we are no longer under the law? Paul says absolutely not. We now live in the power of the Holy Spirit and do what is right because we have yielded all we are to Him. In Galatians 5:16, 18, Paul says, *"I say then: Walk in the Spirit, and you shall not fulfill the lust of the flesh... But if you are led by the Spirit, you are not under the law."* When we are walking in the power of the Holy Spirit, we will want to do what is right and through His power do what the law says we should do. When we try to keep the law in order to live the Christian life or to become a believer, our lives are filled with turmoil and chaos because of the battle raging within. It is impossible to keep the law through our fleshly efforts, and trying to do so is contrary to what the Scripture teaches. However, when we walk in the Spirit, we become more intimate with Jesus. We are dead to the law and married to Jesus as Paul reminds us in Romans 7:4–6

> *Therefore, my brethren, you also have become dead to the law through the body of Christ, that you may be married to another— to Him who was raised from the dead, that we should bear fruit to God. For when we were in the flesh, the sinful passions which were aroused by the law were at work in our members to bear fruit to death. But now we have been delivered from the law, having died to what we were held by, so that we should serve in the newness of the Spirit and not in the oldness of the letter.*

- **We should know we are no longer slaves of the sin nature.**

> *Do you not know that to whom you present yourselves slaves to obey, you are that one's slaves whom you obey, whether of sin [sin nature] leading to death, or of obedience leading to righteousness? But God be thanked that though you were slaves of sin [sin nature], yet you obeyed from the heart that form of doctrine to which you were delivered. And having been set free from sin [sin nature], you became slaves of righteousness.* (Rom. 6:16–18)

NO...I WON'T GO THERE

Paul stated that since we have presented ourselves to Jesus, we should know that we are no longer a slave to the sin nature. When we were obedient and surrendered our all to Jesus, we become His child and are no longer controlled by the sin nature. We are controlled by the power of the Holy Spirit. Before we invited Jesus into our lives and received Him as our personal Savior, we were slaves of sin and obeyed a life directed by Satan. As we look back on this part of our life, we feel ashamed that we ever lived that kind of life. Even now as believers, when we allow our minds to harbor sin and we fall back into the old way of life, we will feel ashamed until we repent of our sin and seek forgiveness. As we learn to say no, we become a slave of righteousness as we progressively become more like Jesus. The closer we live to Jesus, the more intimate we become with Him. When we minister out of our intimacy with Jesus, the joy of the Lord becomes our strength, and there is excitement, energy, and joy in our hearts. This is the choice we now have the power and authority to make. There is no condemnation for us as a believer. We have been set free from the law of sin and death as Paul reminds us in Romans 8:1–2.

> *There is therefore now no condemnation to those who are in Christ Jesus, who do not walk according to the flesh, but according to the Spirit. For the law of the Spirit of life in Christ Jesus has made me free from the law of sin and death.*

Had I been taught these principles when I first became a believer, I feel I would not have battled with overcoming the old sin nature for so many years. Learning and applying these principles to our daily life will result in our developing an intimate worship experience with Jesus every day. When this occurs, the Christian life becomes exciting and is filled with peace, joy, love, and happiness. Learning and applying these principles will take time. However, Paul began teaching them early in the new believer's life. Although these truths may seem unclear when we first hear them, if we ask the Holy Spirit to teach us as we faithfully read and study the Bible, they will become exciting and a part of our life.

The old sinful nature is subservient to the new nature of the resurrected Christ. We now have the authority to say no to the old sinful nature and to yield to the control of the new nature, Jesus Christ. However, it is possible for us to be deceived by the devil and for a time fall into sinful behavior. When this happens, we will feel ashamed and may keep believing the lie of the devil that God will not forgive us. However, God in His mercy will keep reminding us of His forgiveness and love for us. He assures us of this love in 1 John 1:9, *"If we confess our sins, He is faithful and just to forgive us our sins and cleanse us from all unrighteousness."*

We must remember we do not have to fall back into sin. However, if we have not learned to say no to temptations, it is easy to do. When we do, we must recognize it and immediately confess and receive forgiveness so our fellowship with Jesus is restored. Fellowship is essential for an intimate relationship with Jesus.

We must understand the temptation of sin will always be present, and this will occur for as long as we are alive on this earth. The temptation is for us to plug the old sin nature back into our life. We have the choice to yield to the temptation or to say no to it. Paul says do not let sin reign in our bodies, thus stating we have the authority to say no to the temptations of sin. As we learn to bring every thought into the obedience of Christ, the Holy Spirit gives victory over the sin whatever it may be, and we say, "No, I won't go there."

CHAPTER 3

The Baptism and Filling by the Holy Spirit

These two subjects have been referenced in previous chapters. However, it is important to look at them in their theological context in the Bible. This is one of the most misunderstood and controversial doctrines in the Christian church. Therefore, it is imperative for one to understand what the Bible says concerning these important doctrines. The moment one receives Jesus as their personal Savior, they are baptized by the Holy Spirit. There is no salvation experience without the baptism by the Holy Spirit. The Holy Spirit places the unbelieving sinner into the death of Jesus on the cross. Understanding the biblical teaching of the baptism by the Holy Spirit will equip a new believer to live from the position of victory. This is the centerpiece of the salvation experience.

As a young Christian without any specific instruction in how to live this new life, I knew nothing about what the Bible taught concern the baptism and filling by the Holy Spirit. There were those who said we are saved and then baptized by the Holy Spirit. Others said this is a second work of grace accompanied by speaking in an unknown tongue as a sign one has received the Holy Spirit. I was very zealous and wanted whatever blessing God had for me. False advice was given in abundance along with some good sound biblical instruction that kept me from going off the deep end into a sea of heresy.

However, there was a lacking of sound scriptural teaching focusing on the meaning of Acts 2 and the true meaning of the baptism by the Holy Spirit. Therefore, I, along with many others in my generation, was confused by the charismatic movement's teaching that if you are filled with the spirit you will speak in tongues. Through much studying of the scripture, I began to understand that if we do not have the Holy Spirit living in us we are not true believers in Christ. The Bible teaches the Holy Spirit convicts us of our sin, convinces us of the truth of the gospel, and when we say yes, "I believe" places us into the death of Jesus on the cross. At that moment of faith, all the power of the resurrected Christ comes to live in us through the person of the Holy Spirit, never to leave us. This is the baptism by the Holy Spirit. Each day as we yield to His control, He fills us anew with His presence.

It is imperative to see what the scripture has to say and then apply it to our lives. When we do, we will understand God never intended for us to live the Christian life in our own strength. Our understanding the "baptism and filling by the Holy Spirit" is essential for us in knowing what happens in our innermost being when we receive Jesus as our Savior and Lord. The Holy Spirit draws us to the Father, convicts us that we are sinners, convinces us Jesus died for us on the cross and rose up from the grave. When we say yes, "I believe," He places us into the death of Jesus. This is the baptism by the Holy Spirit.

The phrase "baptism by the Holy Spirit" is used only seven times in scripture by four different New Testament individuals.

The First Person Was John the Baptist

John was quoted by all four gospel writers. They all spoke of the same phrase by John.

> *I indeed baptize you with water unto repentance, but He who is coming after me is mightier than I, whose sandals I am not worthy to carry. He will baptize you with the Holy Spirit and fire.* (Matt. 3:11)

> *I indeed baptized you with water, but He will baptize you with the Holy Spirit.* (Mark 1:8)

> *John answered, saying to all, "I indeed baptize you with water; but One mightier than I is coming, whose sandal strap I am not worthy to loose. He will baptize you with the Holy Spirit and fire."* (Luke. 3:16)

> *I did not know Him, but He who sent me to baptize with water said to me, "Upon whom you see the Spirit descending, and remaining on Him, this is He who baptizes with the Holy Spirit."* (John 1:33)

John's promise said when Jesus comes and fulfills His purpose, He will baptize His followers with the Holy Spirit. These four references refer to one and the same experience. This means the power of our sin nature is brought under the death of Christ and we have received His power to live the Christian life.

The Second Person Was Jesus as He Spoke to the Church in Jerusalem

And being assembled together with them, He commanded them not to depart from Jerusalem, but to wait for the Promise of the Father, which, He said, "you have heard from Me; for John truly baptized with water, but you shall be baptized with the Holy Spirit not many days from now." (Acts 1:4–5)

This promise was fulfilled on the day of Pentecost in Acts 2 when the Holy Spirit came to indwell the apostles and the church at Jerusalem.

The Third Person Was Peter Sharing Jesus's Promise with the Gentiles

In Acts 10 Peter was summoned by representatives from Cornelius, a Gentile, to come and interpret a vision he had seen. Peter explained the vision, and Cornelius and his household became believers in Jesus. In Acts 11 Peter shared how they were baptized by the Holy Spirit just like he and the other apostles were in Acts 2.

And as I began to speak, the Holy Spirit fell upon them, as upon us at the beginning. Then I remembered the word of the Lord, how He said, "John indeed baptized with water, but you shall be baptized with the Holy Spirit." If therefore God gave them the same gift as He gave us when

*we believed on the Lord Jesus Christ, who was I
that I could withstand God?* (Acts 11:15–17)

The Fourth Person Was Paul Speaking
to the Church at Corinth

*For as the body is one and has many mem-
bers, but all the members of that one body, being
many, are one body, so also is Christ. For by one
Spirit we were all baptized into one body—
whether Jews or Greeks, whether slaves or free—
and have all been made to drink into one Spirit.*
(1 Cor. 12:12–13)

Paul was explaining how every member of the church is
important whatever their gift or position may be. He told of
how every believer is baptized by the Holy Spirit into the body
of Christ.

Water Baptism Symbolizes the
Baptism by the Holy Spirit

*Or do you not know that as many of us as
were baptized into Christ Jesus were baptized
into His death? Therefore we were buried with
Him through baptism into death, that just as
Christ was raised from the dead by the glory of
the Father, even so we also should walk in newness of life.* (Rom. 6:3–4)

The baptism by the Holy Spirit refers to the placing of
believers spiritually into the body of Christ at the moment of

their conversion. Water baptism is symbolic of this experience. The believing Jews were first baptized into the body of Christ at Pentecost (Acts 1:5 and 2:1–7); the Gentiles were first baptized into the body of Christ at the house of Cornelius the centurion (Acts 10:44 and 11:15–16); and ever since, when a sinner trusts Christ, he or she is made a part of that same body by the baptism of the Holy Spirit and shares it with the church and the world through water baptism. We established this truth in the previous chapter. However, in order to make it clear in our minds, we have repeated some of it again.

The Baptism by the Holy Spirit Occurs at the Cross

The salvation experience begins with the Holy Spirit drawing the sinner to Jesus, and when one says yes to the drawing, convicting, and convincing work of the Holy Spirit, we are baptized spiritually into the death of Jesus on the cross. He died in our place so we can have new life. However, He did not stay in the grave but was resurrected the third day victorious over death and our sin. When we realize it was for our sin that He died and the Holy Spirit convicts us and convinces us of God's love for us, and we choose by faith to believe Jesus rose from the grave, we are transformed by God's love and grace.

The Holy Spirit Comes to Live in Every Believer

When the Holy Spirit baptizes (places) a sinner into the death of Jesus, He indwells the new believer from that time forward. Without the Holy Spirit, one has never been saved.

"But you are not in the flesh but in the Spirit, if indeed the Spirit of God dwells in you. Now if anyone does not have the Spirit of Christ, he is not His" (Rom. 8:9).

The Believer Is to Be Constantly Being Filled with the Holy Spirit

"Therefore do not be unwise, but understand what the will of the Lord is. And do not be drunk with wine, in which is dissipation; but be filled with the Spirit [literally says, "But be constantly filled (controlled) by the Spirit"]" (Eph. 5:17–18).

This is to be our way of life. This is the reason that when we do sin, we must immediately confess it and receive God's forgiveness. This is so we can be filled with the Holy Spirit again. Our sin breaks our fellowship with God, and when fellowship is broken, God will not use us to bless others.

Therefore do not let sin reign in your mortal body, that you should obey it in its lusts. And do not present your members as instruments of unrighteousness to sin, but present yourselves to God as being alive from the dead, and your members as instruments of righteousness to God.
(Rom. 5:12–13)

The Filling of the Spirit Occurs When We Yield All to Jesus

This is not an experience. It is a lifestyle—a lifestyle of confession of sin and yielding to the control of the Holy Spirit in our daily lives.

Remember when we are saved (receive Jesus as our Savior), the Holy Spirit places us spiritually into the death of Jesus on the cross. At that moment, the power of our old sin nature is replaced by the resurrected Christ and we have the freedom and power to say no to the temptation of sin.

Our old sinful nature remains living within us and will try to keep us from remembering the Holy Spirit (the spirit of the resurrected Jesus) lives within us to give us victory over our old sinful nature and its temptations. In the previous chapter, we saw in John 14:16–18 Jesus saying, "I am going away physically so I can come to you in the person of the Holy Spirit." The Holy Spirit is the resurrected Jesus. The old sinful nature is subservient to Jesus who lives in us through the Holy Spirit. When we by faith yield our lives to the control of the Holy Spirit, we walk in the Spirit because we are yielded (surrendered) to His control. We do not have to beg the Holy Spirit to come and be with us for He already abides in us. He is a person, not some mystical form hovering over us. Our intimate relationship with Jesus is essential to be filled with the Holy Spirit.

"But we all, with unveiled face, beholding as in a mirror the glory of the Lord, are being transformed into the same image from glory to glory, just as by the Spirit of the Lord" (2 Cor. 3:18).

There is one baptism by the Holy Spirit, which occurs when we receive Jesus as our Savior, but there are many fillings of the Holy Spirit.

As a pastor and an evangelist, I have experienced many fillings of the Holy Spirit.

Any time a pastor or evangelist preaches the gospel and people are saved, it is because of the filling of the Holy Spirit. In reality, every believer needs to receive a fresh filling of the Holy Spirit each day and for each activity during the day. This should be our lifestyle.

I remember a day back in 1976 when I was leading a revival team in South Korea. I had preached every night for a week and had spent all those days going from house to house sharing the story of Jesus. Many had received Jesus as their personal Savior. On Saturday the missionary had arranged for us to go to the North Korean border and witness on a military base. I was not scheduled to preach, so I did not want to go. I wanted to rest, but God had other plans. The missionary said we needed to go, so my associate pastor, John Randolph, and I represented our team. However, inside I was wishing I wasn't going. Little did I know what God had in store for us on that memorable day. We had lunch with the general of the 12th Division of the South Korean army and he gave us a tour of the DMZ. It was amazing. Then they brought us down from the DMZ about three miles to an installation where about three hundred soldiers were waiting to hear the gospel. Another pastor was scheduled to preach, but the jeep he was riding in had a flat tire, which made them late. We were on a tight schedule, so the missionary came to me and asked if I could preach. My interpreter was with me, so I said yes. When I began to preach, the convicting power of the Holy Spirit fell on us all. It was evident Christ in me was doing the preaching. There were over fifty of the soldiers who received

Jesus as their personal Savior. God had given us such a great service we were later leaving than we had planned.

We had to be back in Wonju for the evening service, so the missionary was hurrying through small villages to get there on time. He was not cleared to be driving because the prior year he was in an accident and was ordered not to drive for a year. For him it seemed like the worst thing possible happened. In one of those little villages, a drunken man wandered into the front fender of the van. He seemed to be hurt, and it happened right in front of the police station, so it did not look good for our missionary. The man was not moving and seemed to be dead. The missionary just sat down on the back of the van and wept. It was possible he could be sent to prison. I did not know what to do, so I put my hands on both of his shoulders and began to pray standing against the devil. I can't remember ever praying like that before. When I finished, a jeep parked beside our van and the chaplain of the South Korean army got out and said, "I will take care of this." (We had been with him on the DMZ.) In a few minutes he came out and said we could go. The drunk man had gotten up and walked away. We got to the church just in time for the service to begin. I walked right into the pulpit and preached. There were several people who trusted Jesus, including a Buddhist who was

104 years old. We had experienced a day with many fillings of the Holy Spirit. It made me ashamed of myself to think I did not want to go. The next morning the chaplain called and told the missionary the police had no record of a drunk being hit by the van driven by our missionary. We had witnessed many miracles of God and what it meant to minister in the power of the Holy Spirit.

In 1967 I was invited to preach a week-long revival meeting in a small church in Mississippi. I arrived on Saturday, and it was very apparent the Holy Spirit was already at work in the church. The services started on Sunday morning with a record attendance of 175 in Sunday school. The Holy Spirit was filling the hearts of the people and they were filling the pews. It rained during the middle of the week and the people still filled the church building. They even had to bring in extra chairs. I preached twice a day at the church building and witnessed one-on-one all day every day. When the week concluded, I was privileged to witness the pastor baptizing sixty-six people who had received Jesus as their personal Savior. We had witnessed a mighty filling of the Holy Spirit's blessing resulting in many changed lives.

As Paul commanded the believers in Ephesus to be constantly being filled with the Holy Spirit, every believer is to live daily in the power of the fresh filling of the Holy Spirit. This is not an experience we seek to have but a lifestyle we must live. The Holy Spirit lives in every believer just waiting for us to allow Him to fill our lives with His presence so He can do His work through us. We never have to beg the Holy Spirit to be with us as some seem to believe. We must confess any known sin and yield our all to His control within us and He will fill us with His presence.

When we are filled with the Holy Spirit, there will be visible evidence of the fruit of the Spirit.

"But the fruit of the Spirit is love, joy, peace, longsuffering, kindness, goodness, faithfulness, gentleness, self-control. Against such there is no law" (Gal. 5:22–23).

Do we possess the evidence of the fruit of the Spirit? The countenance of love, joy, and peace; the conduct of long-suffering, kindness, and goodness; the character of faithfulness, gentleness, and self-control? Our countenance, conduct, and character will be the final test of our being filled with the Holy Spirit.

CHAPTER 4

How We Sin against the Holy Spirit

The last chapter closed reminding believers how we are to live in the fullness of the Holy Spirit. Also how, if we do sin, we must confess our sin agreeing with God we messed up. This is because our fellowship with Jesus is broken and must be restored. It must be restored so the Holy Spirit can use us to reach unbelievers with the good news of Jesus. This chapter will reveal three ways a believer may sin against the Holy Spirit.

Years ago, when I was a young twenty-six-year-old preacher, God began teaching me this lesson. I was a pastor in Texas, when a friend called me from Mississippi and invited me to come and preach a weeklong revival meeting. It was a small church in the Mississippi delta that had 125–150 people in attendance. They had just completed building a new worship center and the pastor wanted to reach people for Jesus and fill it up. However, most of the people had no vision for soul winning and reaching people for Jesus. The services started on Sunday morning with no evidence of the Holy Spirit working in the hearts of the congregation. The spirit of the services was sterile and cold. On Thursday night there had been no moving of anyone coming to Jesus nor any of the church members getting their hearts right with God. It was evident that something was wrong within the fellowship of the church. The Holy Spirit was being lied to, grieved, and quenched all at the same time.

I was a young, inexperienced pastor who did not know any better than to speak out loud what I perceived to be happening in the church. On Thursday night, the first thing I said was this is the coldest church I have ever seen and someone is failing to be obedient to God. That didn't seem to help, and the services continued to be cold all the way through Sunday morning. At the close of the service, no one came to Jesus nor was there any movement among the Christians getting their hearts right with God. We had one more service for the church to be obedient to God. Sunday afternoon the pastor and I spent a lot of time in prayer. Our hearts were burdened for revival to break out in the church. I had gotten to know many of the people, and God spoke to my heart concerning what was taking place in the church. He laid on my heart a message on "how a Christian sins against the Holy Spirit." I shared much of what I am writing here. During the invitation, the Holy Spirit began to move on hearts. One man stood up and began to walk to the back of the church building. I didn't know what was happening when another man at the back of the church started down the aisle toward him. I recognized them as two leaders in the church. When they met, they fell into each other's arms and began to weep. They were seeking each other's forgiveness. Then I saw two ladies (wives of these men) get up and come to each other, falling into each other's arms seeking forgiveness. Then all of them came to the pastor sharing how they had been at such odds they would not even speak to each other. The Holy Spirit was no longer grieved, and people all over the building began to go to each other getting their hearts right with God and each other. This continued for forty-five minutes. The church was no longer cold.

The service had already lasted for almost two hours, and I did something I had never done before or since. I asked everyone to sit down and I preached another sermon. I shared how we had been there a whole week and no one had been saved. I preached a short message on how one comes to Jesus and gave another invitation for souls to be saved. There were six people who came forward trusting Jesus. When the church got their hearts right

with God and each other, the Holy Spirit was
free to do His work through His church.

Jesus lives in every believer through the person of the Holy
Spirit. It is important for us to understand the reality of this
relationship and how we, through our disobedience, sin against
the Holy Spirit.

In the previous chapter we saw how being filled with the
Holy Spirit is a must for us to fulfill our ministry as a believer
and to live in joy and peace. When we sin against the Holy
Spirit, it is impossible for God to bless us as individual believers
or collectively as members of our local churches. In order for
God to bless His churches in fulfilling the Great Commission,
it is imperative that we live in fellowship with the Holy Spirit.
When we are out of fellowship with one another, the Holy Spirit
is lied to, grieved, or quenched, resulting in a spiritual climate
where it is almost impossible for anyone to be saved.

God has chosen to use the believers in His churches to
reach lost humanity with the saving message of Jesus. However,
when we as believers are more concerned about doing what we
want and think, resulting in our disobedience to the will of God
for our lives, we sin against the Holy Spirit.

We have seen in earlier chapters how God brings an unbeliever to salvation through the drawing, convicting, and convincing power of the Holy Spirit. When church members are
living in sin, there will be few or no one being saved. God will
not use a church or an individual believer living in rebellion and
sinning against the Holy Spirit.

Understanding the Holy Spirit's Role in the Believer

- **He indwells the believer.** Every believer is bought and paid for by the blood of Jesus. From the moment Jesus is invited into our life, the Holy Spirit takes up residence.

> *Or do you not know that your body is the temple of the Holy Spirit who is in you, whom you have from God, and you are not your own? For you were bought at a price; therefore glorify God in your body and in your spirit, which are God's.* (1 Cor. 6:19–20)

Many times I have heard someone pray at a Christian gathering, "Oh, Holy Spirit, come and be with us at this meeting." I want to stand up and shout, "He is already here! He came with me!" As a believer, we never have to ask the Holy Spirit to come and be with us. The moment we invite Jesus into our life, the Holy Spirit baptizes us into the death of Christ on the cross, and from that moment until we die, He lives within our body. We need to be sure we have confessed our sin and surrendered our hearts to the Holy Spirit's control every day. Remember—if we do not have the Holy Spirit, then we have never been saved.

> *But you are not in the flesh but in the Spirit, if indeed the Spirit of God dwells in you. Now if anyone does not have the Spirit of Christ, he is not His.* (Rom. 8:9)

- **He guarantees our salvation.** Once we have received Jesus into our lives, He never leaves us. The Holy Spirit seals us and guarantees our salvation. We may sin and our hearts will grow cold, but it is not because He has left us. We have broken fellowship with Him.

   In Him you also trusted, after you heard the word of truth, the gospel of your salvation; in whom also, having believed, you were sealed with the Holy Spirit of promise, who is the guarantee of our inheritance until the redemption of the purchased possession, to the praise of His glory. (Eph. 1:13–14)

The presence of the Holy Spirit is the guarantee of our salvation. He is not only the agent of our salvation; He is the One who gives us the assurance of our salvation experience.

- **He empowers us for service.** It is impossible to serve our Lord through our efforts of trying harder. We must yield our hearts to the Holy Spirit's control and allow Him to work through us.

   But you shall receive power when the Holy Spirit has come upon you; and you shall be witnesses to Me in Jerusalem, and in all Judea and Samaria, and to the end of the earth. (Acts 1:8)

In Acts 1, Jesus gave the promise of power when the Holy Spirit comes upon the believers. In Acts 2, this promise was fulfilled as Peter, along with all the believers, witnessed with great power, and three thousand unbeliev-ers became followers of Jesus. The same Holy Spirit lives in every believer today to empower us to do whatever He leads us to do. We cannot live the Christian life and do ministry in our own strength. If we try to do so, we will fail. Witnessing of God's grace in the energy of the flesh grieves the Holy Spirit. When we sin against the Holy Spirit, our intimate relationship with Jesus is broken and must be restore through confession.

As stated previously, there are three sins named in the New Testament that a believer commits against the Holy Spirit. We can lie to, grieve, or quench the Holy Spirit. We will now define how these sins affect our lives.

The First Sin Is Lying to the Holy Spirit

Lying to the Holy Spirit is pretending to do or be some-thing we are not. In plain language, it is being hypocritical. We say one thing and then do another. Ananias and Sapphira were examples of hypocrites.

> *But Peter said, "Ananias, why has Satan filled your heart to lie to the Holy Spirit and keep back part of the price of the land for your-self? While it remained, was it not your own? And after it was sold, was it not in your own control? Why have you conceived this thing in your heart? You have not lied to men but to God." (Acts 5:3–4)*

Ananias and Sapphira pretended to be something they were not. They were examples of the first hypocrites in the church in Jerusalem. After the day of Pentecost in Jerusalem, there were thousands of new believers in Christ. Many of them had lost their means of making a living and others were away from home. Members of the church who had property sold it and gave the proceeds to the apostles to distribute to those who had physical needs. Ananias and Sapphira seemed to like the attention the people were getting who were making gifts. They also had property to sell, but they were selfish and greedy. Therefore, they conspired together to sell their property and say they sold it for a big price but to hold back some of it for themselves.

For example, they may have sold it for a $1,000, but they said they were giving it all when they gave $500 to the apostles. They pocketed $500 for themselves. However, they did not realize God knew what they had done and revealed it to Peter. Peter asked them, "Why has Satan filled your heart to lie to the Holy Spirit and keep back part of the price of the land for yourself?" Peter said they had the freedom to keep part of the price if they wanted to, but to lie and say they were giving it all was not acceptable. Their lie cost them their lives and set an example to the early church, resulting in thousands being added to the church in Jerusalem.

As believers in Jesus, we will never become perfect as long as we live on this earth, but we are to grow in our relationship and be honest with God. When we mess up, our hearts need to be made right by admitting and confessing our sin to God. Our intimate relationship with Jesus must grow and be maintained daily.

I never shall forget a comment one man
made after I had baptized him and several

others. He had lived a rough life. At one time he had worked as a bartender and did his own bouncing of unruly patrons. He had been gloriously saved, and I had the privilege of baptizing him and his two sons the same night. After we had finished the baptismal service, he came by and shook my hand and said, "Oh, Preacher, I don't know what to say. All I know is you are just a helluva preacher." I was not offended by his statement but felt highly complimented. He had not yet learned how to talk like a Christian, but he was being honest before God.

Many times we as Christians know the right things to say, but in our hearts we are thinking wrong.

In order for us to not lie to the Holy Spirit, we must be honest with God.

The Second Sin Is Grieving the Holy Spirit

We grieve the Holy Spirit by doing or saying things we should not do or say. All bitterness, wrath, anger, evil speaking, malice, etc. must be confessed and put away from us. We must be kind and forgive others as God has forgiven us or we grieve the Holy Spirit.

> *And do not grieve the Holy Spirit of God, by whom you were sealed for the day of redemption. Let all bitterness, wrath, anger, clamor, and evil speaking be put away from you, with all malice. And be kind to one another, tender-*

hearted, forgiving one another, even as God in Christ forgave you. (Eph. 4:30)

Remembering how God has forgiven us is the foundation for our being able to forgive. Our right relationship with God is essential for our being able to forgive others. This principle was demonstrated by the church spoken of at the beginning of this chapter. Bitterness and an unforgiving spirit had been growing for a long period of time. It was only after the two men, who were leaders in the church, got their hearts right with God that they were able to forgive each other. When this happened, it spread throughout the whole church. The Holy Spirit was no longer grieved and God's blessings poured out on the church by the people getting their hearts right with God and each other resulting in unbelievers being saved. The people's hearts were filled with the Holy Spirit and the love of Jesus. The Holy Spirit was no longer grieved and the peace of God filled their hearts.

Once we understand how it is possible for us to grieve the Holy Spirit, we become quick to confess our sin in order to get our hearts back in fellowship with God. Any kind of unchristian speech or attitude will grieve the Holy Spirit.

> *Let no corrupt word proceed out of your mouth, but what is good for necessary edification, that it may impart grace to the hearers.* (Eph. 4:29)

The Third Sin Is Quenching the Holy Spirit

Paul also told believers not to quench the Spirit or put out the Spirit's fire. This occurs when the Holy Spirit speaks to a believer and is leading them to something He wants them to do.

"Do not quench the Spirit" (1 Thess. 5:19 NKJV). *"Do not put out the Spirit's fire"* (NIV).

We grieve the Holy Spirit when we do or say something we should not do or say. Quenching the Holy Spirit is just the opposite. It is failing to do what the Holy Spirit may lay on our hearts to do. For example, the Holy Spirit may impress us to tell someone how much Jesus loves them and we refuse to do it. We have quenched the Holy Spirit. The Holy Spirit may convict us about our need to begin to tithe to our church or give a certain amount to the church's building program and we say no—the Holy Spirit is quenched. When this occurs, our hearts turn cold and we feel God is far away from us, resulting in our becoming very miserable people. Any time the Holy Spirit leads us to do something and we do not do it, we quench the Holy Spirit and our fellowship with God is broken and needs to be restored.

I remember a time when I was preaching in a revival meeting and God was blessing with many souls being saved. We had morning services with a lot of sweet testimonies of how God was blessing the hearts of the people. During one of these services, the spirit of the meeting went from hot to cold and sweet to sour. I knew immediately when it happened but did not know why until the next morning. The Holy Spirit had been moving in our lives and suddenly was quenched. The next morning a sweet, precious, older lady revealed why the service had turned cold the previous morning. She said, "I have a confession to make. Yesterday morning God laid on my heart to share a testimony of what

He was doing in my life. I rebelled and did not do what God told me to do. I confessed it to Him and I want you to forgive me as well." She then shared what God had told her to share, and the sweet spirit of the services returned, and our hearts were blessed. The Holy Spirit was no longer quenched.

In the previous chapter, we learned from Paul that as believers we are to be constantly being filled with the Holy Spirit. This is the scriptural norm. In our modern churches, we seem to have a false idea that only the really spiritual can live the spirit-filled life. The truth is every Christian can and should be living the spirit-filled life. All that is required is for each of us to surrender all we are to the control of the Lord Jesus who lives in us through the Holy Spirit. We do this by checking our hearts to see if we have unconfessed sin of lying to, grieving, or quenching the Holy Spirit. In our spiritual maturity, we are not all equal, but we are equal in our ability to surrender all we know about who we are to Jesus each day.

When we do sin against the Holy Spirit, be honest and confess it and we will be filled again with His presence.

CHAPTER 5

Living from the Position of Victory

Learning to live our lives in fellowship with Jesus is the key to walking in the fullness of the Holy Spirit. When we as believers sin against the Holy Spirit, it is impossible to recognize our position of victory in Christ. This position is not something we win but one we receive when we trust in Jesus. We, by faith, begin to rest in this position and allow Jesus to live His life through us. The Bible teaches that when Jesus was resurrected from the grave, He took His position in heaven far above any problem or power and we are seated with Him.

On August 30, 2018, I went to my doctor for an annual checkup. All of my previous checkups had been perfect, so I figured there was nothing to worry about. However, when all the test results were in, the doctor said my cholesterol was above what it should be and I was overweight. She wanted me to quit eating carbs and sugar. Most of my life I had been in pretty good shape and was not overweight. All of my vital signs were well in the range they should be, but now I am older and still eat whatever I feel like eating. The doctor said if I did not do something about the way I ate I could have a stroke. My wife is the best pie maker I have ever seen, and I love pie and ice cream. I came home and told her I had to change the way I had been eating and began to do research on how I should eat. Also I committed my need to our Lord in prayer and began to say no to the things I should not eat. Even through Thanksgiving and Christmas I did not cheat.

It was because Christ in me empowered me to say, "No, I won't go there," in my mind. Six months later I went to see my doctor and she was elated. I had lost thirty pounds, and my cholesterol was half of what it was six months before. After a year and six months has passed, I still am walking in victory. My blood work is great, and my weight is stable where it should be. Through yielding to the power of the resurrected Christ living in me through the Holy Spirit, I am able to say no to whatever my temptation may be.

In Ephesians 1 and 2 Paul reminds us God has bestowed on us all the power that it took to bring Jesus forth from the grave. We are sitting together with Christ in the heavenly places, above all problematic defeats, temptations, and difficult circumstances. We are living from a position of victory. When we appropriate this truth by faith, we begin to live in the power and strength of Jesus who lives His life through us. Paul explains this truth in Ephesians 1 and 2.

> *...and what is the exceeding greatness of His power toward us who believe, according to the working of His mighty power which He worked in Christ when He raised Him from the dead and seated Him at His right hand in the heavenly places, far above all principality and power and might and dominion, and every name that is named, not only in this age but also in that which is to come.* (Eph. 1:19–22)

> *But God, who is rich in mercy, because of His great love with which He loved us, even when we were dead in trespasses, made us alive together with Christ (by grace you have been saved), and raised us up together, and made us sit together in the heavenly places in Christ Jesus.* (Eph. 2:4–6)

Whether our problem is being overweight from eating the wrong things or being enslaved by some habit, we overcome by resting by faith in Christ from the position of victory.

We Are to Live from the Position of Victory

As believers we are seated with Jesus in heavenly places far above everything which hinders us or tempts us. This is our spiritual position. Whether it is depression, lust, overcoming a sinful habit, or overeating resulting in being overweight, we renew our minds and say, "No, I won't go there." Whatever the problem, habit, or temptation may be, we yield our hearts afresh to the control of the Holy Spirit.

Jesus makes it clear we are to abide in Him, for without Him we can do nothing. Paul makes it clear in Ephesians 1 and 2 that we are seated with Jesus in heavenly places, resting in Him far above all principalities and powers. As a new believer we are not to do anything until we understand what Jesus has already done. We are to seek His will and know He will enable us to do it. Failing to learn this lesson will result in our trying to work for Jesus in the flesh, resulting in burnout and other failures.

When Jesus came to live in our bodies, all the power of the resurrection came with Him to enable us to live from the position of victory. This is why we can say, "No, I won't go there," to temptations and walk victorious in the Holy Spirit. I was able to apply this principal to eating what the doctor wanted me to eat.

Victory Was Won at Calvary—Not by Something We Can Do

We are conditioned to think we must do something to win the victory. However, Jesus has already won the victory when He came forth from the grave. In Watchman Nee's book, *Sit, Walk, Stand: The Process of Christian Maturity*, he states, "Our crucifixion with Christ is a glorious historic fact. Our deliverance from sin is based not on what we can do, nor even on what God is going to do for us, but on what He has already done for us in Christ. When that fact dawns upon us, and we rest back upon it, then we have found the secret of a holy life."[5] He goes on to tell the following story:

> An engineer living in a large city in the
> West left his homeland for the Far East. He

---

5   Watchman Nee, *Sit, Walk, Stand: The Process of Christian Maturity.*

was away for two or three years, and during his absence his wife was unfaithful to him and went off with one of his best friends. On his return home he found he had lost his wife, his two children and his best friend. At the close of a meeting which I was addressing, this grief-stricken man unburdened himself to me. "Day and night for two solid years my heart has been full of hatred," he said. "I am a Christian, and I know I ought to forgive my wife and my friend, but though I try and try to forgive them, I simply cannot. Every day I resolve to love them, and every day I fail. What can I do about it?"

"Do nothing at all," I replied.

"What do you mean?" he asked, startled. "Am I to continue to hate them?"

So I explained, "The solution of your problem lies here, that when the Lord Jesus died on the cross He not only bore your sins away, but He bore you away too. When He was crucified, your old man was crucified in Him, so that that unforgiving 'you,' who simply cannot love those who have wronged you, has been taken right out of the way in His death. God has dealt with the whole situation in the cross, and there is nothing left for you to deal with. Just say to Him, 'Lord, I cannot love, and I give up trying, but I count on Thy perfect love. I cannot forgive, but I trust Thee to forgive instead of me, and to do so henceforth in me.'"

The man sat there amazed and said, "That's all so new, I feel I must do something about it." Then a moment later he added again, "But what can I do?"

"God is waiting till you cease to do," I said. "When you cease doing, then God will begin. Have you ever tried to save a drowning man? The trouble is that his fear prevents him trusting himself to you. When that is so, there are just two ways of going about it. Either you must knock him unconscious and then drag him to the shore, or else you must leave him to struggle and shout until his strength gives way before you go to his rescue. If you try to save him while he has any strength left, he will clutch at you in his terror and drag you under, and both he and you will be lost. God is waiting for your store of strength to be utterly exhausted before He can deliver you. Once you have ceased to struggle, He will do everything. God is waiting for you to despair."

My engineer friend jumped up. "Brother," he said, "I've seen it. Praise God, it's all right now with me! There's nothing for me to do. He has done it all!" And with radiant face he went off rejoicing.[6]

It goes against human nature for us to forgive someone who has hurt us. Within our own strength and understanding we are

---

[6] Ibid.

unable to do it. When we try to put hurt feelings aside and forgive someone who has hurt us, without committing it totally to Jesus and allow Him to forgive through us, we will fail.

We Must Rest by Faith in Our Position in Christ and Seek His Will for Our Life Each Day

The first thing we need to do after we have received Jesus into our life is to draw near to Him and rest in His presence. We must learn to trust Him in every situation. Our lives are filled with unusual difficult circumstances and unforeseen things that present the opportunity for worry or concern. When we learn to live from the position of victory, we can face life's difficult circumstances with praise and thanksgiving. Worry will be replaced with peace and joy as we learn to rejoice in the presence of Jesus.

In 2018 I was scheduled to preach on Sunday morning at a church in Bakersfield, California. I was all prepared to preach, but about 3:00 a.m. I woke up feeling sick at my stomach, and every time I would lie down I would get sick again and throw up. I went into the living room and tried to sleep in my recliner. I finally quit throwing up and went to sleep. When I got up I was weak and didn't know how I would have strength to preach. By faith and with the help of my dear wife, I got dressed and drove to the church not knowing what would be the outcome, but knowing from experience when I am the weakest God is strong within me. I preached with power and freedom. God's anointing was present and God's people were into the message. They would not let me stop preaching. After preaching for almost an hour, I felt stronger than when I began.

By faith, I was seeking to abide in God's will for my life even when I did not feel well. It was not I but Christ in me.

Living from the position of victory enables us to deal with difficult circumstance and worry through rejoicing in the Lord and giving thanks in all things.

As we read Paul's writings, we come to understand the Christian life is about learning to rest in the Lord Jesus until He reveals His will. This is hard for us to do because our world is focused on our doing something in order to be productive. However, God wants us to learn to rest in Jesus until He reveals His will. In Watchman Nee's little book, *Sit, Walk, and Stand,* he does a short commentary on the book of Ephesians. He says we must learn to sit with Jesus before we can walk, and when we learn to walk, we must learn to stand against the wiles of the devil. All of this is a part of our sanctification process.[7]

It is very important to spend time in God's word each day so the Holy Spirit can remind us what God says concerning our old sinful nature and its temptations. If possible, I like to do it first thing in the morning, which enables me to say, "No, I won't go there," to temptations. Whatever our temptation may be, we apply the same truth of overcoming. I can hear some of you saying, "I don't have time in the morning." I understand how daily schedules vary. However, the point is spending time with Jesus every day. We may have to go to bed earlier so we can get up an hour earlier to

---

[7]   Ibid.

spend time with our Lord. Each one of us is different and has different schedules, but it is imperative we find time alone each day with God. For me I find going to bed earlier enables me to get up at least by 4:00 a.m. so I will have time to read God's Word and pray before I begin the other activities of the day.

Each morning is begun by purposefully yielding our hearts, minds, and bodies to our Lord in prayer. Our will must be surrendered to Christ who lives in us through the Holy Spirit. Time must be spent in God's Word each morning so the Holy Spirit can remind us what God says concerning our old sinful nature and its temptations. If we can't do it in the morning, we should read the scripture the night before and yield our hearts afresh in the morning. All of these spiritual exercises are essential for us to live from the position of victory. When difficult circumstances are not understood, we must rejoice in our relationship with Jesus. Think about who Jesus is within us and trust Him, by faith, to deal with our difficult circumstance. Remember all of our sins were covered by the blood of Jesus at Calvary. As we begin to rejoice and thank God for all Jesus has done, our hearts will fill with joy and victory. We will be comforted with peace in the midst of our difficult circumstance. An intimate personal relationship with Jesus must be continued throughout each day. Do what Paul says in 1 Thessalonians 5:18, give thanks unto our Lord in everything.

In everything give thanks: for this is the will
of God in Christ Jesus for you. (1 Thess. 5:18)

This truth became very real to me one Tuesday morning as I was driving to the weekly pastor's breakfast and fellowship. On the way to the meeting place, there is a left-turn light where the traffic is heavy and gets backed up. This morning the traffic seemed heavier than usual. Cars on my right were passing me and then cutting in front of other cars before they got to the light. By this time my blood was beginning to boil. These people were infringing on my rights.

As I began to get more angry, the Holy Spirit reminded me of the verse I had read earlier in the morning, "Let your gentleness be evident to all." It could not have been clearer to me if He had spoken verbally and said, "Are you being gentle?" I replied, "No, Lord," but I am saying no to that attitude right now. At that moment all the built-up anger begin to drain out of me and I relaxed in the presence of Jesus and His peace filled my heart.

I thanked the Lord then and many times since for the unusual circumstance which helped in beginning to teach me this truth. Little did I know this was just the beginning of the lesson. This lesson has continued through later experiences. When we walk in the spirit, our hearts will be filled with the fruit of the spirit and Jesus will bring His love to our difficult circumstance. It is through difficult circumstances God teaches us the essentials of living from the position of victory. Whatever circumstance we face, the love of Jesus living through us will always be sufficient. Remembering the following four principals will enable us to live from the position of victory.

- **First, we will face some type of difficult circumstance each day.**

This is the reason we must have a daily intimate relationship with Jesus. It is impossible to cope with the circumstances of life without allowing Jesus to live HIs life through us. God expects us to learn to live from the position of victory. Paul gives us the secret formula in Philippians 4:4–7:

> *Rejoice in the Lord always, Again I will say, rejoice! Let your gentleness be known to all men. The Lord is at hand. Be anxious for nothing, but in everything by prayer and supplication, with thanksgiving, let your requests be made known to God; and the peace of God, which surpasses all understanding, will guard your hearts and minds through Christ Jesus.*

- **Second, rejoice in the midst of difficult circumstances.**

When we do not understand our difficult circumstance, we must rejoice in our relationship with Jesus. This was so important to Paul he said it again. Often we do not understand why things happen in this life. We do not understand the sudden death of a loved one or why our baby dies without warning. On and on go the difficult circumstances of life. What are we to do? We are to think about who Jesus is within us and trust Him, by faith, to deal with our difficult circumstance. Remember we are seated with Him in heavenly places. Circumstances change, but Jesus never changes, and He loves us with an unfailing love. As we begin to rejoice and thank God for all Jesus has done, our hearts are filled with joy and victory.

- **Third, do not worry about anything.**

> *Therefore I say to you, do not worry about your life, what you will eat or what you will drink; nor about your body, what you will put on. Is not life more than food and the body more than clothing?* (Matt. 6:25)

Jesus taught that we are not to worry about anything pertaining to life. We are to trust Him for food, drink, and clothes to wear. Jesus taught we are to trust Him for everything; Paul said be anxious for nothing. Yet our mind is constantly finding things to be concerned about. We need to cast all of our cares upon Him because He cares for us.

- **Fourth, bring everything to our Lord in prayer with thanksgiving.**

When we are tempted to worry or have a critical spirit, we can say, "No, I won't go there." This is a type of prayer. It should be our first reaction to whatever our difficult circumstance may be. When the negative thought comes to our mind, we say no and renew our mind in the presence of Jesus. When we do, we can begin to be thankful and praise the Lord in the midst of our problem.

In 1 Thessalonians 5:16–18 Paul says, *"Rejoice always, pray without ceasing, in everything give thanks; for this is the will of God in Christ Jesus for you."*

Remember, we are to live from the position of victory. It is God's will for us to rejoice, pray without ceasing, and give thanks in the difficult circumstance. Paul said give thanks in everything. I remember a time when a lady in our church said to me, "Preacher, you mean I am to thank God for my problems?"

I said, "No, if a truck runs over your husband and kills him, you are not to thank the Lord he is dead, but you are to rejoice in being able to bring your hurt to Jesus in prayer and to give thanks for His comfort in meeting your need." All of this is true, but I should have said yes, we are to give thanks in all things, which includes our problems.

Jesus is always with us to meet our needs, and it is His will for us to rejoice in Him, pray without ceasing, and to be thankful for His presence and grace in the midst of our difficult circumstance. When we haven't grown in our relationship with God, we have trouble saying no to negative thoughts that flood our minds.

Therefore, when trying circumstances come, many blame God and can't even pray, much less rejoice and be thankful for His love and comfort. This is because we haven't learned how much God loves us. Also, we haven't grown up in Christ and know very little about what it means to have an intimate relationship with Him.

I have learned through many years how God teaches us new lessons throughout our lives. When we begin to learn something new, He gives us opportunity to put it into practice. I have shared some of these already in this writing. As I am writing on how to live from the position of victory, an entirely different type of temptation has attacked my mind. I have had times when words flowed freely as I typed, but there are other times when the thoughts go into a deep freeze and nothing comes out. (I am sharing my innermost personal thoughts.) When this happens, I am tempted to get down on myself. The devil whispers in my ear and says things like, "You are completely inadequate as a writer. You really have nothing new to share, or why don't you have a pity party." When this happens, I am learning to rejoice in my relationship with Jesus, stand against worry, and begin giving thanks for God's love and goodness to me. I say, "No, I won't go there," to the devil's whispers. Joy fills my heart, and as Paul says, the peace of God guards my heart and mind in Christ Jesus. We must, by faith, remember to stand in our position of joy and victory in Jesus far above all principalities and powers. In ourselves we are inadequate to do anything, but in Christ we can do all things that He desires for us to do. I share these personal thoughts because you will have similar experiences.

Rejoice in the Lord, don't worry about anything, bring all of our needs to God each day with thanksgiving, and the peace of God will guard our hearts and minds in Christ Jesus. As we do this, God will give us peace as He deals with our difficult circumstances, and we will learn through every difficult time God is trying to teach us something good. During the time of this writing, America and the rest of the world are facing the coronavirus pandemic. Fear has gripped the hearts of many around the world. Many immature believers are worried about how they and their families will survive. Although we do not know what the future holds, as believers we know who holds the future and we can rest in Him and give praise for His care and protection. We can give thanks and rest in His comfort, for He cares for our every need. We rejoice and praise His wonderful name even when we may not understand our circumstance.

By faith say no to the temptations of the old sin nature, and we will live from the position of victory already won. Now we move forward to dealing with overcoming temptations.

CHAPTER 6

❦

The Way to Escape from Temptation

One morning, as I was thinking about the way we escape from temptations, my mind went back to Genesis 3 where Eve was confronted by Satan through the serpent. *"Then the serpent said to the woman, 'You will not surely die. For God knows that in the day you eat of it your eyes will be opened, and you will be like God, knowing good and evil'"* (Gen. 3:4–5).

Satan asked Eve about what God had said, and Eve replied, "We can eat of every tree except the one tree in the center of the garden. If we do we surely will die."

Satan, through the serpent, said, "You will not surely die. You will become like God knowing good and evil."

This appealed to Eve and she ate of the fruit and gave some to Adam and he ate it as well. Both of them were disobedient to God, and sin entered into our world because they wanted to become like God. God loves the people of the world so much He sent us Jesus to die for our sin. When we open our hearts and trust Him as our personal Savior, He lives within us to enable us to be obedient and overcome the temptation of yielding our lives to live in sin. We spend the rest of our lives saying no to the temptation of sin and becoming more like Jesus.

When we understand our position of victory in Christ, our approach to overcoming temptations changes. We know Jesus won the victory over sin when He was resurrected from the grave. Now the one who won the victory lives in every believer through the person of the Holy Spirit.

We are seated with Him in heavenly places far above every evil temptation. Therefore, every believer has the power through Christ to say no to the temptations of the devil.

> *Therefore let him who thinks he stands take heed lest he fall. No temptation has overtaken you except such as is common to man; but God is faithful, who will not allow you to be tempted beyond what you are able, but with the temptation will also make the way of escape, that you may be able to bear it.* (1 Cor. 10:12–13)

Paul reminded the Corinthian church to always be on guard against the temptations which were sure to come their way. He pointed out that the temptation to sin is common to every believer, but he also gave the assurance God is faithful to not allow us to be tempted beyond what we are able to bear. God has provided a way to escape the temptation. None of us are without temptations, and many are enslaved by sinful habits. We are instructed to look for the way to escape, not to look for a way to yield to the temptation.

It is my conviction the way to escape is to be obedient to what God tells us in His word—the Bible. Had Adam and Eve been obedient to what God said, they would not have fallen into sin. We are told to resist the devil by saying no to his temptations and to bring every thought into the obedience of Christ.

Paul reminded the church at Corinth concerning the sins of their forefathers, the nation of Israel. He pointed out they were committing the same sins as their forefathers.

In our present-day churches we face the same sins and temptations. We lust after prestige, power, sex, idols, and other fleshly desires. Therefore, we must learn to deal with the temptations of the flesh. As Paul wrote to the church at Ephesus, he reminded them of who Christ is living in them. We are reminded of the greatness of the power of the resurrected Christ living in us through the Holy Spirit. We are seated together with Jesus far above all principality and powers and every name that can be named. We do not have to yield to the temptation to sin. To be tempted to sin is not a sin.

The Way of Escape Begins in Our Minds

Temptations come in many forms. However, we can be sure they are common to all of us as human beings. There is no temptation I have that you may not have, and there is no temptation you have that I may not have. They are common to us all, but there is a way to escape the temptations. The way to escape begins in our minds.

> For though we walk in the flesh, we do not war according to the flesh. For the weapons of our warfare are not carnal but mighty in God for pulling down strongholds, casting down arguments and every high thing that exalts itself against the knowledge of God, bringing every thought into captivity to the obedience of Christ, and being ready to punish all disobedience when your obedience is fulfilled. (2 Cor. 10:3–6)

In Romans 12:1–2 and in his second Corinthian letter, Paul gives us directions concerning the importance of the use of our minds.

We are to renew the thoughts of our minds and bring every thought into the obedience of Christ.

On Wednesday, October 9, 2019, Robin Lee Covington posted on Baptist Press an article titled "Taking Every Thought Captive." She is the wife of Dr. Randy Covington who is the executive director of the Alaska Baptist Convention. They were formerly missionaries to Russia for the International Mission Board of the Southern Baptist Convention. She writes of the traumatic time when they arrived in Russia as missionaries. She said,

> As a brand-new missionary, I basked in the glow of living out my dream of ministering overseas in Russia. I knew many faithful people were praying for me. Praying the prayer, "God bless and protect the missionaries." Suddenly that glow shattered when two colleagues, a husband and wife, were murdered. Brutally and cruelly. I'll never forget the face of the young man who came to tell us that these precious servants had been found dead in their apartment. My gut reaction was immediate. "God if this is what you sent me here for, I didn't sign up for this, I didn't come here to die!" And instantly, shame shattered my heart. I was appalled at my thoughts.

She goes on to explain how she and her family had to learn to take every thought captive to the obedience of Christ. They were living in the apartment where the murdered couple had lived and everywhere they looked they were reminded where the dead couple lay and where their blood was splattered on the walls. They overcame the negative thoughts by thinking on Philippians 4:8 and the things which were true and noble.

When they had learned to bring every thought captive to the obedience of Christ, God used them to lead many students to trust Jesus as their personal Savior.[8]

Our Minds Are Attacked with the Desires of Our Sinful Nature

"Let no one say when he is tempted, 'I am tempted by God'; for God cannot be tempted by evil, nor does He Himself tempt anyone. But each one is tempted when he is drawn away by his own desires and enticed" (Jas. 1:13–14).

- **First, we think wrong thoughts**

The desires of the sinful nature, when yielded to, cause us to think wrong thoughts. All of these wrong thoughts begin in our minds and have the potential of becoming sinful actions. Jesus said if a man or woman lusts in their heart for one of the opposite sex, they have committed adultery in their hearts already. Sinful thoughts always lead to sinful actions if they are not dealt with in our minds. Our temptations come through the mind as we are enticed like a fisherman uses bait to catch a fish. Satan uses the bait of our sin nature to get us to yield to temptation. This is

---

8   Robin Lee Covington, "Taking Every Thought Captive," Baptist Press, October 09, 2019, http://www.bpnews.net/53724/firstperson--taking-every-thought-captive.

why we must take every thought captive and bring it into the obedience of Christ before we take the bait and sin. We do this by saying no to the wrong thought and yielding to Jesus in prayer. For example, when we are tempted to feel unloved and unwanted, we recognize it to be a lie of Satan and say, "No, I am not allowing my mind to go there." When tempted to look with lust on the opposite sex, we say, "No, I won't go there in my mind."

When tempted to eat something we know will be bad for us and cause us to gain weight, we say, "No, I am not eating that." All of these are pitfalls the devil uses to tempt us in our mind. We must always beware of self-pity, self-preoccupation, or feeling inadequate causing us to want to give up. When these occur, we must say, "No, I won't go there."

- **Second, we must yield to the power of the Holy Spirit**

Whatever we may be tempted with by Satan, we will overcome as we yield to the power of the resurrected Christ who lives in us through the Holy Spirit. Satan has the victory over our minds only because we do not know we possess the power to resist him, by saying no to his temptations and bringing our thoughts into captivity to the obedience of Christ. When we are filled with the Holy Spirit, we have the power to walk in obedience. We learn these things as we study the scriptures. In Luke's gospel chapter 4, we find the story of Jesus being led by the Holy Spirit into the wilderness where He spent forty days in prayer and fasting.

Then Jesus, being filled with the Holy
Spirit, returned from the Jordan and was led by

the Spirit into the wilderness, being tempted for forty days by the devil. And in those days He ate nothing, and afterward, when they had ended, He was hungry. (Luke 4:1–2)

Satan came to Jesus and tempted Him three more times, and each time Jesus answered him with words from the Bible. (Satan had already tempted Him for forty days.) Jesus was hungry, so Satan gave Him a rock and tempted Him to turn it into bread.

But Jesus answered him, saying, "It is written, 'Man shall not live by bread alone, but by every word of God.'" (Luke 4:4)

Then Satan offered Jesus all the kingdoms of the world if He would bow down and worship him. Jesus answered him in Luke 4:8: "And Jesus answered and said to him, 'Get behind Me, Satan! For it is written, "You shall worship the Lord your God, and Him only you shall serve."'"

Jesus was then taken to the pinnacle of the temple in Jerusalem. Satan challenged Jesus to jump off and ask the angels to catch Him, but once again He answered with scripture: "And Jesus answered and said to him, 'It has been said, *"You shall not tempt the Lord your God"*'" (Luke 4:11).

In verse 1 of Luke 4, the scripture says Jesus was filled with the Holy Spirit. We as believers are to be filled each day with the Holy Spirit, and as we yield all we are to Him, we have the power to resist the wiles of Satan. When we read the word of God every day, the Holy Spirit gives us answers in how to resist the devil and his temptation.

Another weapon in this battle is to memorize scripture and hide it in our heart so we will not sin against God.

> *Therefore submit to God. Resist the devil and he will flee from you.* (Jas. 4:7)

> *I beseech you therefore, brethren, by the mercies of God, that you present your bodies a living sacrifice, holy, acceptable to God, which is your reasonable service. And do not be conformed to this world, but be transformed by the renewing of your mind, that you may prove what is that good and acceptable and perfect will of God.* (Rom. 12:1–2)

- **Third, be transformed by the renewing of our minds**

We have the authority to renew our minds. Paul tells us in Romans 12 we are transformed by the renewing of our minds. One of the biggest problems in our churches today is with our Christian young people who believe the lies of Satan about their self-worth. (This is true of adults as well.) They believe the lies of feeling no one loves them or cares whether they live or die and are tempted to take their own lives because they begin to live in depression. If they fail to say no to the lies, they may end up taking their own life. We must renew our minds. When we read and study the Bible every day, we understand Jesus loved us enough to die on the cross for our sin and we sit spiritually with Him in heavenly places far above all the evil which attempts to lie and deceive us. When we know the scripture, the Holy Spirit gives us victory so we can answer with the Word of

God. It is imperative we show our children they are loved, and as they yield to the control of Jesus in their lives daily, they can bring every negative thought into the obedience of Christ. Through the power of His resurrection they can say no to every negative thought. We must learn to say, "No, I won't go there," when wrong thoughts pop into our minds—bringing these thoughts into captivity.

Renewing Our Minds Will Enable Us to Overcome Worry and Fear

Therefore I remind you to stir up the gift of God which is in you through the laying on of my hands. For God has not given us a spirit of fear, but of power and of love and of a sound mind. (2 Tim. 1:6–7)

There is no fear in love; but perfect love casts out fear, because fear involves torment. But he who fears has not been made perfect in love. (1 John 4:18)

Therefore do not worry about tomorrow, for tomorrow will worry about its own things. Sufficient for the day is its own trouble. (Matt. 6:34)

Paul reminded us God has not given us the spirit of fear but has given us the power of love and a sound mind. John taught the perfect love of God casts fear out of our minds. Jesus said we are not to worry about tomorrow for tomorrow will take care of its own trouble. Worry always seems to follow fear.

When we are fearful, we worry about what made us fearful. We glean from the scripture all worry and fear is sinful. How are we going to overcome this sin?

When I was a young boy still in elementary school, on occasions my parents would go shopping in towns larger than where we lived. We lived in the country on a farm, so I had to ride the school bus home and would get home before they did. Sometimes they were later than what I thought they should be and fear would grip my heart and I would begin to worry. My mind would play all kinds of tricks on me. I would worry about the possibility of them having an accident and what would happen to my brother and me if something happened to our parents. When we allow fear and worry to run through our minds, the devil has a wonderful time with our minds, and mine was no different. I would run to the door and look down the road to see if they were coming. This would go on for what seemed like hours. Finally they would arrive home and I felt so relieved.

The next time they would be gone this same story would rerun. I never shared this story with anyone, so I never received any outside help to overcome my fear and worry. As I grew older, I became more mature and braver in dealing with this problem. However, it was still in the back of my mind. When I went off to college, I became more self-sufficient, but in the back of my mind there was still the old fear and worry. During the second semester of college I surrendered my life to God and the gospel ministry. I began to learn what it meant to surrender my fears and worries to God and to walk by faith. Before my last year of college, Lois and I got married. We were sure this was God's will for us and believed He would take care of our needs. Lois had graduated and had a job making a dollar an hour. I was pastor of a small church that paid me twenty-five dollars a week. I had another part-time job, so we thought we were set. We rented a small apartment and paid the first month's rent. After we paid the meager expenses for the wedding, we had twenty-five dollars in our pockets with another twenty-five coming from the church on Sunday. I tell you all this to say God had brought me past all the worry and fear. That has been the story of our marriage. We find and seek to do whatever God's will is for us and trust Him to take care of us. We can honestly say He has always cared for us, so we refuse to be fearful or worry about anything. I am not saying we are never tempted, but I am saying when we are, we say, "No, we are not going there." Then the peace of God fills our hearts.

We Must Make an Intentional Choice

Each morning we must surrender to the control of the resurrected Christ through the Holy Spirit. This is a choice we must intend to make. Jesus lives within us and desires for us to let Him determine the direction our life will take each day. When the old sinful nature tempts us with thinking wrong thoughts, which will produce wrong actions, we must choose to say no to these thoughts. We have the power to do this through yielding to the Holy Spirit's control. When by faith we say no to temptations, the power of the resurrected Christ gives victory over the temptation or habit that seeks to enslave us. As we renew our minds by remembering these truths, our lives are transformed by the Holy Spirit.

> *So I say, live by the Spirit, and you will not gratify the desires of the sinful nature. For the sinful nature desires what is contrary to the Spirit, and the Spirit what is contrary to the sinful nature. They are in conflict with each other, so that you do not do what you want.* (Gal. 5:16–17 NIV)

When We Are Tempted by Habits, We Can Escape by Saying No and Pulling Down Strongholds

Christ who lives in us through the Holy Spirit gives us victory over the temptation or habit that has enslaved us. Most new believers have some kind of stronghold in their lives when they become a Christian. Strongholds are determined by whatever one is a slave to when they become believers. Because Christ lives in us, we possess the power to bring every craving in our minds to the obedience of Christ. Day by day, hour by hour, and moment by moment strongholds are broken and pulled down.

This is true of the strongholds of alcohol, drugs, tobacco, sex, food, or whatever the stronghold may be. Remember, the power of the resurrected Jesus lives in us enabling us to say no to any habit that has us enslaved. First we say, "No, I won't go there," and second we present the stronghold to Jesus so He can tear it down. Here are some of the possible, most common strongholds in today's society.

- **It may be alcohol addiction.**

    While I was in the seminary, I pastored a small church located in the foothills of the Sierra Nevada mountain range. There was a man and his wife who were members and very faithful servants. They shared with me a testimony I have never forgotten. Before they were saved, they were both alcoholics. They drank a fifth of whiskey every day. God delivered them from that addiction as they learned to bring every thought to the obedience of Christ and began to say no to the temptation. This stronghold in their lives was broken.

- **It may be drug addiction.**

    This remains an ongoing problem in our society. However, for the believer in Christ, there is deliverance as they say no and yield their mind to the control of the Holy Spirit.

- **It may be tobacco addiction.**

    I know a man, when convicted of this truth, overcame the use of tobacco. He had used it for about thirty-five years and overcame it by saying no to the temptation and yielding himself to the control of Jesus who lives in him through God the Holy Spirit. Once he made the choice to say no, God gave immediate deliverance.

Every time the desire returned, (according to his testimony) he continued to say no and to trust Jesus, and has yet to use it again. The stronghold was torn down.

God gave the victory. This principal is true no matter what the temptation or habit may be. We must say no to our selfish desires.

- **It may be a sexual addiction.**

  We live in an era when it seems common for couples to live together before they are married. They seem to think sex should be experienced before marriage. Many seem to have multiple sex partners before marriage, not realizing an addiction is being formed that will have to be overcome.

- **It may be our appetite for food.**

  I shared earlier how I had to overcome my desire for food that was not healthy for my body.

We could go on and on listing various strongholds, but whatever your stronghold may be, there is a way to escape. We yield our all to Jesus and say no to the temptation, bringing every thought into the obedience of Christ.

From chapter 1, we have seen a progression in our Christian life moving us toward Jesus becoming our life.

CHAPTER 7

Jesus Is Our Life

In our previous chapters, we have seen how we become a believer in Jesus and how we move in a progression to become like Him. Through this spiritual growth process, He literally becomes our life. Although this wonderful truth has taken a life time to learn, the principle has been planted in my heart since I first surrendered my heart to the lifelong call to the gospel ministry. When at twenty-two years of age, by faith, my dear seven-months-pregnant wife and I left our home in Texas to enter seminary in California. Neither of us had ever been to California, and both of us had only been out of Texas on one other occasion. Then six years later with two precious little girls ages three and five, we, by faith, left a secure pastorate in Texas to move to Nevada to start a new church. We had no promise of any salary, but Jesus was really becoming our life, and we were trusting Him. The following story will explain more of what I mean.

In 1965, we were pastoring a church in Texas when God called our family to Elko, Nevada, to pastor a mission and to establish

a Bible-preaching church. We responded
with complete faith believing this was God's
will and that He would meet our needs. We
had no promise of a salary. He did care for
every need. Four days before we were scheduled to move we had no money for moving.
On our last Sunday night before we were to
load up and leave on Monday morning, God
had provided the money with which to move
through various churches and friends.

It was indeed a miracle. We worked hard
and God did bless. However, physically I was
wearing out. In order to live and pay bills, I
painted houses and did other odd jobs. Also,
Lois and I led in building a first unit church
building and parsonage. I was preaching five
or six times a week plus doing Bible studies in three or four different venues. I was
committed and I was sincere in what I was
doing. Much activity was substituted for living in and being led by the Holy Spirit. I was
involved in what I thought I needed to do
without getting a word from God about how
He wanted me to do it. There is altogether a
difference in ministering in the energy of the
flesh and the energy of the Holy Spirit. However, at that time I had not learned the difference. God took what effort He could use and
blessed. It is amazing how when we try to do
His work He blesses what He can. However,
my body paid the price because I had not
learned the lesson of resting in the presence

of Jesus until He showed me what He wanted to do through me. This was all new to me. There was too much of me trying and not enough of Him working through me. After twelve years of this seven-day-a-week fleshly work, I burned out. Through much waiting, resting, and recovery, I have learned God has a better way—yielding to His will and working through His strength. Even with all of my weaknesses, wrong decisions, and inabilities, God took our efforts and blessed with many souls being saved and discipled. Through these experiences, I learned something of what it meant for Jesus to be my life. I learned when yielded to His will, He gives the strength and energy to do His will.

It is common to hear someone say, "He or she is my life." This is said by wives about their husbands, husbands about their wives, and parents about their children, and grandparents about grandchildren. What we mean is that we love the person about whom we are speaking so much that our whole purpose in life is to do things that please them. However, when is the last time you heard someone say, "Jesus is my life"? When Jesus is our life, we can say no to the temptation of sin, and our total desire is to please Him. How does this come to pass in our lives?

"The thief does not come except to steal, and to kill, and to destroy. I have come that they may have life, and that they may have it more abundantly" (John 10:10).

First, We Surrender Our All to Jesus

Jesus came to give us life and life more abundant. He came to live His life through every believer. When we receive Him as our personal Savior, He calls us to surrender our all to Him. We can't live the Christian life in our own strength, but He can be in us only what we allow Him to be. He wants to be our everything.

"Jesus said to him, 'I am the way, the truth, and the life. No one comes to the Father except through Me'" (John 14:6).

When we come to Jesus, He changes our lives. In John 3 He says we are born again spiritually. The Holy Spirit causes us to want to know God and experience what it means to have eternal life. He convinces us of the truth of what Jesus did for us on the cross and of the power of His resurrection. He convicts us of our sin and of our need to be forgiven.

In that moment we cry out to God in belief and ask Him to save and forgive us. The Holy Spirit places us spiritually into the death of Christ on the cross, and the power of our old sin nature is overcome and we are set free from the control and power of our sin nature. The spirit of Christ now lives within our bodies through the Holy Spirit. The power of the resurrected Christ now lives within our lives. For many people, Jesus is someone who is thought of only on Sunday. However, He lives in every believer and desires to bless and direct his/her life every day. We can do all things through Christ who is the strength within us. God's desire is for us to yield daily to Jesus and allow Him to live His life through us.

Second, We Choose Daily for Jesus to Be Our Life

"Likewise you also, reckon yourselves to be dead indeed to sin, but alive to God in Christ Jesus our Lord. Therefore do not let

sin reign in your mortal body, that you should obey it in its lusts" (Rom. 6:11–12).

Remember—the power of our old sin nature has become subservient the moment we receive Jesus into our lives; however, our old sin nature is still alive and well living within us. Now we have the freedom and power to choose to yield our will to the control of Jesus who lives within us. Without our making the conscious choice of yielding to the Holy Spirit's control, we will yield to the control of our old sin nature. This is why Jesus must be our life. Through Him we can do all things. We must focus on our intimate, personal relationship with Him. Without Him living His life within us, it is impossible to think right or to do what He desires for us to do.

In Romans 6, Paul reminds us to count on as a fact that we died to the sin nature when the Holy Spirit baptized us into the death of Christ on the cross. God is always working in our lives as believers to transform us into the image of Jesus. He is always teaching us new things. Life has become our classroom of learning to be like Jesus.

From March 2016 through mid-March 2017, my wife Lois and I ministered to the First Baptist Church in Tehachapi, CA, as their interim pastor. We traveled the fifty miles up the mountain every Sunday and Wednesday through all kinds of weather. However, the weather wasn't the biggest obstacle; it was the lines of trucks and slow cars driving in the wrong lanes. These revealed a real flaw in my character which I thought had been corrected through an earlier circumstance. (Earlier lesson continued) They infuriated me when they pulled out in front of me and slowed me down. I would jokingly say something about it to the church on Wednesday nights. It soon became something we joked about often. On my birthday they gave me a golf ball with a car trying to pass a truck on one side and on the other a symbol of the devil. They told me when I got frustrated with the truckers to take the ball to the golf course and knock the devil out of it. We all had a good laugh. This was because they could identify with me. However, over a short period of time, God used this to reveal to me my need to overcome this temptation and to be patient with others. God never wastes an opportunity to teach us a lesson about flaws in our character. I repented of my sin and yielded it all to Jesus who lives in me by the Holy Spirit.

God immediately gave me peace and joy in our drive to Tehachapi. I confessed my sin to the church and God begin to convict many in the congregation of how they felt the same way I had felt. They too began to have victory over their feelings as they yielded their hearts to Jesus as they drove to and from Tehachapi.

When we live in an intimate relationship with Jesus, we experience victory in all circumstances, although at the time victory may seem far from reality. Once again God had taught me a new lesson as I yielded my heart to Jesus. Don't be discouraged if you do not completely learn the lesson the first time around. God loves us enough to keep working with us until we learn the lesson. However, it will be a lot more pleasant for us if we learn it the first time. This is a part of our sanctification.

Third, Keeping a Set of Rules and Trying Harder Always Fails

My parents were fine Christian people, but they grew up in an era where being a good Christian was judged more by what one does not do or what one does to determine if one is a good Christian. They would not allow a deck of cards to be in our house, but they had no convictions against playing dominoes. As one can see, I was raised in a legalist view of being a Christian. I had a lot of hang-ups to overcome.

Often we get the cart before the horse. We approach discipleship by setting up a set of rules or things we need to do in order to be a good Christian. Many of these things are good and essential for our spiritual growth. However, without realizing it, we move from our relationship of grace to a doctrine of works.

We move from depending on Jesus to live His life in us to something that appeals to our old nature, and before we know it, we are depending on something we think we can do to live the Christian life. We are saved by God's grace and we must live the daily Christian life by God's grace. The things we do must come out of our daily love relationship with Jesus. When He is our life, we have no problem giving or serving, because all we are and possess are surrendered to Him.

When Jesus is our life, we will want to read the Bible and pray. We will want to come to church and fellowship with other believers. Because of our daily walk with Jesus, He leads us in the things we do, and we will rejoice in Him and experience His joy, peace, and strength. We are motivated by our intimate relationship with Jesus. We desire to be in the center of His will for our lives, and whatever His word reveals concerning His will, we will want to do. The end results will be our serving through the strength of Christ who lives His life in us.

Fourth, When Jesus Is Our Life, We Will Rest in the Position of Victory

When difficult circumstances come our way, we rejoice in Jesus. When Jesus is our life, we realize we think right and do right because He is controlling our daily walk. We must yield our will to His control moment by moment each day. This is easier when everything is going the way we think it should, but when things are not going well for us, our faith is tested. We must constantly be reminded of what Paul said, "Rejoice in the Lord always." Jesus desires for us to have daily intimacy with Him that is not determined by good or bad circumstances.

He wants us to rejoice and trust Him no matter what our circumstance may be.

When most of us face unpleasant situations in life, the first thing we do is to become anxious. We allow worry to control our minds and actions. Paul says we must learn to bring our worries to Jesus and trust Him to care for our needs. When we do, our hearts and minds are filled with peace and joy. The answer to overcoming unpleasant circumstances is found in learning to give thanks unto our Lord and rejoicing in His name by faith. Never forget Paul's instruction in Philippians 4:4–7:

> *Rejoice in the Lord always. Again I will say, rejoice! Let your gentleness be known to all men. The Lord is at hand. Be anxious for nothing, but in everything by prayer and supplication, with thanksgiving, let your requests*

be made known to God; and the peace of God,
which surpasses all understanding, will guard
your hearts and minds through Christ Jesus.

Our family had a vivid reminder of this truth when
our granddaughter, Kristen Hicks, gave birth to our second
great-granddaughter. The following story is the account of a
very unpleasant circumstance.

Our great-granddaughter Avery Hicks
was born November 30, 2011. The doctors
immediately knew something wasn't right
with her heart. They arranged for her to be
airlifted to UCLA Medical Center in Los
Angeles, California. When she was just over
a week old, the doctors said she had to have
open-heart surgery. It was a tense time for
parents, grandparents, great-grandparents,
the entire family, and friends.

There was a large family gathering in the
waiting room as we all waited to hear from
the doctors about the results of the surgery.
When they finally came out after several
hours, they said she had a lot of problems to
repair. When they closed her up, her heart
quit beating and they had to take it out and
manually massage it to start it again. The
doctor said, "We just have to wait and see
how she responds." Her parents and all of
the family were terrified. I remember walking down the hall with our daughter (Avery's
grandmother) and sharing with her how we

must commit Avery into God's hands and trust Him to take care of her. We all knew this is what we should do, but now we were faced with doing it. Her heart lay on her chest for about ten days before the doctors could put it back in her body. It was touch-and-go for many days, but through God's grace and mercy, she slowly began to heal. After eighty-two days in the hospital, she was able to come home. As I write this, she is now over eight years old and has had more surgeries, but now she is sweet, precious, healthy, and full of energy although there may always be issues. Through these difficult circumstances, our family has learned something more about what it means for Jesus to be our life and to rejoice in His name. It certainly doesn't mean we will never have any more heartaches, but when we do, He holds our hands and walks with us through them.

On the second anniversary of Avery's surgery, her mother, Kristen Hicks, posted the following article on Facebook.

Well, today is a very special day in our house. December 8, 2011 will be embedded in our hearts and minds. Today marks 2 years since Avery's open heart surgery, the most terrifying day of our lives.

I wanted to share some intimate details of that day just to remember how truly special she is and more importantly how BIG our

God is! Surgery was over and the repair went beautifully, and then there was the dreaded but...as they were wheeling her out of the OR everything stopped. She was gone, they had to rush back in giving her teeny little heart (the size of a walnut to be exact) manual compressions in order to bring her back. Nothing could've prepared us for this news. Her surgeon said things like, "We are going to do the best we can for her, but right now we just don't know," and, "If at any point I feel like we are hurting her I will tell you." When a top-notch pediatric heart surgeon at UCLA says things like that you know this is serious stuff. We spent the rest of that day pleading for God to keep her here with us, but also knew that ultimately she was His child and if it was His will to take her home to Him we would surrender to that. Needless to say, it was a long day which turned into a very long night. We were living minute by minute not knowing if she would make it through the night, and at that point no one could give us an answer. The fear of the unknown was the worst part. Well, obviously, not only did He keep her here, He also fully restored her life. Today she is a prefect little 2-year-old that runs and plays and even yells NOO, haha! The goodness of God's love is overwhelming. Even in our darkest days, He never left us. That is the best part about trusting in Christ. He's always there no matter what. He doesn't promise for life to be perfect or without suffering, but what He does promise is to be there in the pits of life, holding our hand, giving us the strength to press on. We are so thankful for our precious girl and all that He has taught us through her. Today we celebrate her life and rejoice in the abundant blessings we have received.

Our granddaughter and her husband, along with all of our family, grew and learned through this trying time.

When Jesus is our life, no matter what the circumstances may be, we rejoice in God's grace and love for us. We do not worry but bring everything to Him in prayer and allow him to guard our hearts and minds and give us peace. We do this in the hard times as well as the good times. When a loved one is facing death, our faith is put to a real test as to whether Jesus is our life. It reminds us of what Jesus said in John 11:25–26 to Martha: *"Jesus said to her, 'I am the resurrection and the life. He who believes in Me, though he may die, he shall live. And whoever lives and believes in Me shall never die. Do you believe this?'"*

These words were spoken to Mary and Martha when their brother Lazarus had died. Jesus performed a miracle and brought Lazarus out of the grave, reminding us of how Jesus is our resurrection and life bringing us out of our spiritual death into eternal life. For every believer He lives within us with all the power of the resurrection giving us victory over sin and temptation. This passage also tells us that we too must learn to deal with the heartache of loved ones dying. Because of sin, death has entered into our world, but Jesus conquered death when He was resurrected victorious from the grave. As a believer, the spirit of the resurrected Jesus lives in us to be our life so we can deal with the death of loved ones in a positive and victorious way. When both my parents died, my heart was broken by their loss. Their desire was for me to conduct the funeral services. Through the presence of my living Lord, an unpleasant experience turned into one filled with love, joy, and peace. This is one of the reasons Jesus desires to be our life, so He can live His life in us through the sufferings and heartaches of life.

Satan tempts us through our old sin nature, and we must recognize it and immediately renew our minds and say no to the temptation. This is always a subtle work of Satan. Our sin nature wants us to think of ourselves and react in a sinful way that protects our old self. When that occurs, we must say, "No, I am not letting my mind go there." When the devil tempts us through our old sin nature, he whispers in our ear and says, "God won't really see you through this hard time." Our response must be, "No, I won't go there." The Holy Spirit immediately gives us victory. Jesus is the first one we come to with our difficult circumstance when He is our life. We will be willing to do whatever He leads us to do. We will be at peace in our hearts even when we do not know how God will accomplish what He has asked us to do.

> *I beseech you therefore, brethren, by the mercies of God, that you present your bodies a living sacrifice, holy, acceptable to God, which is your reasonable service. And do not be conformed to this world, but be transformed by the renewing of your mind, that you may prove what is that good and acceptable and perfect will of God.* (Rom. 12:1–2)

When Jesus is our life, He is living His life in us through the presence of the Holy Spirit. We love, think, and live like

Jesus because we are allowing Him to live His life through us. Our hearts are to be transformed by the renewing of our mind.

Throughout this writing, we have sought to lay out the journey of the Christian life from beginning to end. Paul reminded the church in Corinth to prepare for the day when they would stand before the judgment seat of Christ. Here they and we will give an account of how life is lived here on Earth. It is a judgment of reward or loss.

Rewards for those who have lived well and loss of reward for those who have not grown and matured in Christ. It is not a judgment of condemnation to determine whether one will get into heaven or not, but a judgment of blessing for those who have allowed Jesus to become their life.

"For we must all appear before the judgment seat of Christ, that each one may receive the things done in the body, according to what he has done, whether good or bad" (2 Cor. 5:10).

In this writing we have considered how Jesus set the pattern for our early Christian faith and how the New Testament church baptizes and instructs new believers in their walk with Jesus. A spiritual battle can be expected as we learn to overcome the old sin nature. We have seen how water baptism is symbolic of the baptism by the Holy Spirit when the Holy Spirit immerses the unbeliever spiritually into the death of Jesus on the cross. As one comes out of the water, the beautiful picture of the resurrection is portrayed by the new believer. Now as the new believer yields to the indwelling Christ, the filling of the Holy Spirit is experienced. However, when we sin against the Holy Spirit by lying to, grieving, or quenching Him, our fellowship with Jesus is broken and must be restored by confessing our sin. Because we have the power of the resurrected Christ living in us, we begin our new life from the position of victory, seated together with Jesus in heavenly places. Even though we have this position of victory, we are tempted by the old sin nature, but a way of escape is provide by our saying, "No, I won't go there," to the temptation. Through this journey we learn to yield our all to Jesus so He becomes our life as we live each day here on this earth. There will be times in our spiritual growth when we will need to revisit these truths. For example, when we drift from the New Testament pattern, we must return and apply its principles to get back on track. All these principles are basic to our Christian growth and must be continuously applied, but we must never forget to focus on our intimate relationship with Jesus.

When the Holy Spirit baptized us spiritually into the death of Christ on the cross, we died to the power our old sin nature had over us. By faith we sit with Jesus in heavenly places from the position of victory. Because of who Christ is in us through the Holy Spirit, we have the authority to say no to the temptation of sin. When Jesus is our life, we live with joy, peace, and victory in our hearts, whatever the circumstances of life may be.

Remember, when we are totally surrendered to Jesus, we are filled with the Holy Spirit. When we are filled with the Spirit, we walk and live in His power; thus, producing the fruit of the Spirit. The countenance of love, joy and peace, the conduct of long-suffering, kindness and goodness, the character of faithfulness, gentleness, and self-control will be expressed in our lives. Our countenance, conduct, and character will be the final test of our being filled with the Holy Spirit and Jesus being our life.

It is my earnest prayer that the thoughts and experiences shared in this book will enhance your understanding of how much God loves you and who you are in Christ.

APPENDIX

———— ✺ ————

In order for you to understand who you have become in Christ, go back to the introduction and memorize the seven-fold process for coming to Jesus. Understanding this seven-fold process for coming to know Jesus will become a life-changing experience. As wonderful as it is, there is so much more you can expect to happen in your life. For additional study, let me encourage you to go through each chapter and find the answers to the questions asked in each chapter. You can use this method for a continual Bible study.

Chapter 1
The Early Days of Our Faith

Questions to consider:

1. How does one become a believer in Jesus?
2. Why is a new believer instructed to be baptized?
3. What does water baptism symbolize?
4. What is the pattern for spiritual growth a new believer should follow?

Chapter 2
Expect an Ongoing Inner Battle

Questions to consider:

1. What two questions must a new believer answer to live in victory?
2. What part does the new believer's identification with the death and resurrection of Jesus play in overcoming the old sin nature?
3. When does a new believer die to the power of the old sin nature?
4. Why is a new believer dead to the law?

Chapter 3
The Baptism and Filling by the Holy Spirit

Questions to consider:

1. When is a believer baptized by the Holy Spirit?
2. When is a believer filled with the Holy Spirit?
3. Why must a believer walk in the Holy Spirit?
4. How many times is a believer filled with the Holy Spirit?

Chapter 4
How We Sin against the Holy Spirit

Questions to consider:

1. How does a believer lie to the Holy Spirit?
2. How does a believer grieve the Holy Spirit?

3. How does a believer quench the Holy Spirit?
4. When a believer sins against the Holy Spirit, what should he or she do?

Chapter 5
Living from the Position of Victory

Questions to consider:

1. What does it mean to live from the position of victory?
2. When does a believer receive this position of victory?
3. What are the four principles that enable a believer to live from the position of victory?
4. Why should a believer learn to rejoice in the Lord in the midst of difficult circumstance?

Chapter 6
The Way to Escape from Temptation

Questions to consider:

1. Why must a believer understand how Jesus won the victory over sin when He was resurrected from the grave?
2. What part does quoting scriptures play in a believer's overcoming?
3. Where does every temptation begin?
4. What are the three things believers must do when Satan attacks our minds?
5. How does a believer overcome sinful habits and pull down strongholds?

Chapter 7
Jesus Is Our Life

Questions to consider:

1. What is the four-fold process for Jesus to become the believer's life?
2. Why must believers surrender all to Jesus every day?
3. What does it mean for the things a believer does in serving Jesus to come out of his or her intimate relationship with Him?
4. How should a believer react to the hard circumstances of life?

BIBLIOGRAPHY

Covington, Robin Lee. "Taking Every Thought Captive," *Baptist Press*, October 9, 2019.

Fisher Fred L. *The Church: A New Testament Study*. Mill Valley, California: Golden Gate Baptist Theological Seminary, 1959.

Hicks, Kristen. "Second Anniversary of Avery's Surgery." Facebook, November 30, 2013.

Nee, Watchman. *Sit, Walk, Stand; The Process of Christian Maturity*. Fort Washington, Pennsylvania: CLC Publications, 2015.

Wuest, Kenneth Samuel. *Wuest's Word Studies from the Greek New Testament For the English Reader*. Vol. 2. Grand Rapids: Eerdmans, 1997.

CPSIA information can be obtained
at www.ICGtesting.com
Printed in the USA
FSHW011020170821